Words from a Distance

My ramblings in print !

D xxx

Edited by Amina Alyal
Judi Sissons

Stairwell Books //

Published by Stairwell Books
161 Lowther Street
York, YO31 7LZ

www.stairwellbooks.co.uk
@stairwellbooks

ISBN: 978-1-913432-41-6

Cover design by Deborah Ripley
Cover Image ©Heather Curwen
P5

Published by Clarewell Books

www.clarewellbooks.co.uk
@clarewellbooks

ISBN 978-1-913432-41-6

Cover design by Dunn to Perry
www.image-designs.human

Table of Contents

'*Words from a Distance* does what all good writing does, dissolves time and space, flings open doors and windows and makes, in the words of John Donne, one little room an everywhere. The pieces in this anthology were created in the confines of the pandemic but their writers draw on their own experiences and imaginations to conjure our whole world, its landscapes and childhoods, its beauty and brokenness, its could-have-beens and might-still-bes. Here, we have prose and poems, formal and experimental writing, close observation of daily life and flights of imagination. Everything, that is, that makes us human. These fifteen writers, who were thoughtfully guided by Judi Sissons, approach similar themes from different perspectives, so the writers are in conversation with each other, singing like the birds did during those strange, still months when we were unable to get close to each other. The book is beautifully curated by Judi Sissons and Amina Alyal, with images that are arresting, often surprising, and add another dimension to the authors and their writing. *Words from a Distance* is the antithesis of lockdown. It's an opening-up, a bearing-witness, it's shouting from the rooftops and whispering to a trusted other, saying, yes, we're here and we have something to say.'

Victoria Field

Introduction

Words from a Distance was conceived one chilly morning in March 2020 a few days before the national lockdown was announced. I have my friend Rebecca to thank for supporting the idea in its first incarnation. As we stood shivering in our communal gardens, trying to maintain social distance – was it one metre or two – we discussed our options now all our freelance work had been cancelled and panic-buying of loo rolls had set in.

With my own sense of isolation and fear about the virus growing, I figured there would be others feeling at least as anxious as myself, I needed to connect and do something useful. So a writing for wellbeing workshop in our back garden to support the local community seemed like a grand idea. I posted flyers on the noticeboards of our block of flats and had a few enquiries over the next week or so, but it soon became clear that the restrictions and the miserable weather would make this unworkable. Having recently discovered the wonders of Zoom, I decided to move the project online and quickly realised that I could reach out far beyond the local neighbourhood.

As cases of coronavirus rose dramatically and the WHO declared a pandemic, the collision between human rights and public health brought issues of basic human dignity to the fore. We were all at a distance, be it two metres, thousands of miles or the width of a pane of glass between ourselves and our loved ones, and yet we could connect and share our words with others from all over the world.

There were reports of nature recovering due to reduced pollution and images of deserted urban landscapes filmed by drones. On my daily walks through the traffic-free city I stopped to listen to previously unheard birdsong in the trees along empty streets, and Bette Midler's song, 'From a Distance' came to mind.

... From a distance
There is harmony
And it echoes through the land
And it's the hope of hopes ...

The *Words from a Distance* workshops would focus on writing for wellbeing, offering people a chance to gather online, to record their experiences, process thoughts and feelings, or simply to escape them for a while in the company of others, sharing writing and supportive discussion with no critique of the writing.

Writing together has been shown to reduce anxiety, strengthen our sense of community, promote resilience and wellbeing – all of which felt urgent at that time of imposed social isolation. I particularly wanted to offer women a safe space to find their voice and develop their creative writing.

The first of a series of seven workshops took place on 16 April 2020 with ten participants. Keen to establish what they hoped to gain from the sessions, I asked the writers to respond to the statement 'Why I write.' These are some of the reasons they came up with:

- [because] writing is like holding secrets, as yet uncovered, that are twinkling in a corner waiting to be fully revealed
- to have a stronger sense of self
- because I need to process alone
- because I don't want to forget
- to capture the beauty
- to feel real
- to pause the world
- to express myself without fear of judgement
- because I enjoy my brain - the way it plays
- because it's another way to travel and explore
- because language fixes the moment, the scene, the feeling
- to revisit the distant and more recent past
- to articulate my ideas, without my emotions blocking my voice
- [because] time stands still when I write
- because I enjoy performing

My initial assumption that the group would want to write about the pandemic and the minutiae of life under lockdown soon gave way to the realisation that they wanted to write about a wide range of topics. I drew on my own interests and covered everything from myth, psychology, masks and self identities, clothes, personal symbols and significant objects, rituals, psycho-geography, landscape and the natural world, as well as significant world events.

Adapting some of my well-used writing prompts and finding new ones that worked for the online space was an enjoyable challenge. For example, I have a collection of genuine shopping lists, retrieved from supermarket shopping trolleys in the pre-pandemic world. Does anyone write shopping lists on paper now? Previously, I would hand these out at workshops in the real world. Now I scanned the lists into the computer and screen-shared them, inviting the writers to choose one and develop a character and a scenario. There's often a lot to be gained from the type of paper, the handwriting, other little scribbles and notes on the paper, what is left out or crossed out and why? A couple of the shopping list stories have made it into the book.

As the uncertain months of Covid lockdowns dragged on, the weekly sessions continued and became an important focus in our otherwise restricted lives. Thursday mornings found me seated at my computer, coffee and notes at the ready, waiting for the familiar chimes as members of the writing group entered the waiting room for the Zoom meeting. Eager faces would appear on the screen as the writers greeted each other. How's the family? The weather where you are? Are we all safe and well? We would have ten minutes of social chat before we got down to the playful and serious business of writing together. We usually started with a grounding exercise, letting go of anything that wouldn't serve us in the workshop. Then a short free-writing exercise in response to a prompt, to loosen the muscles of hand and brain, because writing by hand keeps the hand-brain super-highway connected.

Free-writing can produce surprising results and creative imagery but can also take the writer by surprise, unleashing powerful, sometimes difficult feelings. The issue of how to create a safe space online was of paramount importance and we spent time at the start of the course sharing our hopes and fears and setting clear boundaries for the group. The group space provided the writers with the opportunity to reflect on their lives, to connect with each other, to re-connect with their remembered selves, writing about profound, amusing and sometimes traumatic experiences. Although we were going nowhere, we travelled great distances together, sharing inner and outer journeys. The writing that emerged in the workshops was often raw and heartfelt.

Technical issues presented problems for some and, despite attempts to overcome this, we unfortunately lost a couple of writers along the way as the challenges of technology made it impossible to find solutions. New people joined the group as the months went on, from all parts of the UK and one woman from as far as Afghanistan.

Over the low point of a cancelled 2020 Christmas I was looking for a way to keep our spirits up. The writers were keen to develop their creative writing skills and the idea of producing an anthology emerged as a way to give us all something to aim for. The opportunity to see their work professionally published would encourage the writers to produce work of a high standard whilst celebrating the spirit of creative friendship and support that had emerged among the attendees.

This would not have been possible without the support of my co-editor, Amina Alyal whom I met through NAWE (National Association of Writers in Education) and a women's online writing network. I was delighted when Amina agreed to work with me on the *Words from a Distance* anthology, sharing her editing expertise and experience of publication. It has been a great pleasure to work alongside her.

To prepare writers for submitting to the anthology, we devised a short course of three workshops on Revising and

Editing to run in January 2021. Anyone who had attended the workshops during 2020 was invited to take part in the course to help them revise and polish work in progress and take their writing to the next level. During each session there was a chance to work on a chosen piece of work with an option to submit up to five pieces to be considered for inclusion in the *Words from a Distance* anthology. Amina attended the first session and delivered a presentation and practical exercise, providing the group with a fascinating insight into the editing process. We particularly appreciated seeing the development of some of her own poems through various drafts - an inspiring and helpful demonstration that gave us all a boost to keep working on our writing.

Marilyn Chandler in her book *A Healing Art* discusses the therapeutic power of writing about our lives, and outlines three stages, or layers of the writing process – introspection, retrospection and transformation. The stages correspond with the form the writing usually takes. Early, expressive writing in a journal or notebook will most likely be **introspective**, purgative, often written from within an experience when the writer is immersed in exploration. Such writing is usually private and not intended for sharing. The **retrospective** stage is reconstructive, perhaps written from a particular vantage point, looking back and beginning to see the shape of an experience, making meaning from it. The writer is beginning to consider structure and analysis. This writing is more likely to be shared with others, in a writing group for instance. A further, **transformative** stage occurs when artistic motives overtake the therapeutic. The writer achieves an aesthetic distance from the subject matter and memory gives way to imagination. According to Chandler, 'Writing begun as therapy will, continued, tend toward art. Therapy is the beginning of healing; art can be its completion.' The confidence and desire to share one's stories with the world signifies the metamorphosis from subjectivity to authorship. All this fed into the processes of writing and editing the writers eagerly took on, with the resulting finished pieces as collected here.

Much of the writing in the book draws on challenging episodes of the writer's lives – childhood, parenthood, relationships, death and bereavement – floods and oceans are contended with, homes and houses hold off-beat perspectives, dreams, and memories. But these are pieces of their times, and come out of lockdown, with all its potential for reflection, and out of this age of environmental urgency, so that themes of the environment and nature are tinged with our particular sense of responsibility and value. Women's lives, warm, poignant or even abusive, are examined with voices wry, light, deeply felt or blisteringly honest. Monuments and power are examined again in light of the times we live in. Food is celebrated. Travel, perhaps nostalgically, comes to the fore. Childhood and school gets a particularly strong range of writing. And finally there is some space given to imagining private paradises and ideals.

Huge thanks are due to Deborah Ripley, who has contributed her design expertise, time and enthusiasm, and to Heather Curwen for her visceral cover image, making this book a work of art. And I am grateful to all the writers who attended the workshops over the past eighteen months, a period that has shown us our vulnerability and demonstrated our resilience and resourcefulness in supporting ourselves and each other. Meeting together to share words with a bunch of gutsy, creative women every Thursday morning has been a joy. At the time of writing, *Words from a Distance* workshops continue to run on a weekly basis.

Judi Sissons
www.thewritingspace.co.uk

'From a Distance' lyrics quoted with permission from Julie Gold.

Amina Alyal

Amina Alyal has published poetry in journals and anthologies, and two collections, *The Ordinariness of Parrots* (Stairwell Books 2015) and *Season of Myths* (Indigo Dreams Publishing 2016), and academic publications. She works at Leeds Trinity University, and runs the open mic Wordspace. She was editor of *Dream Catcher Magazine* in 2020.

Acknowledgements:
'Regeneration' was first published in *All is Flux*, edited by M. B. Gerlach, J. L. Rushworth, J. M. Young and Oz Hardwick (Indigo Dreams Publishing 2020); 'In a Glass Darkly' in *Lighting Out*, edited by Rebecca Bilkau (Beautiful Dragons Collaborations 2021); 'Space Bubble' in *The Spaces Between Us*, edited by Kathleen Morgan, Jamie Stewart & Oz Hardwick (Indigo Dreams Publishing 2021); 'Inferno: Ghosts in the Machine' in *Divining Dante*, edited by Paul Munden and Nessa O'Mahoney (Recent Work Press 2020); 'Purgatorio: On the Verge' and 'Paradiso: Reeds' online at Divining Dante (adobe.com): https://t.co/T78IWxpNm0?amp=1

Regeneration

The thick stink of humanity dispersed,
mellow billowing breezes
bump up against cold cobwebbed brick.
First comes a raven
walking down the middle of a street,
then foxes congregate.
Wild garlic sprouts from the pavement
and last comes a bear, arms full of lilies,
its shadow adamant in the hot noon sun. //

In a Glass Darkly

In a dark room, under an obscure light,
images swim out onto white squares,
and that's how it works, like a brain,

with the planet, and bees each know
only their own wax walls, but hold in mind
the mingling cobwebs of where they have been.

Particles of us pass through pixelated screens,
shedding little drops of honey, oozing.
Each bee is a neuron, each part of a hive.

What if, what if. What if we could speak
to someone the other side of the globe,
hear them say, Come, listen to our music.

We have only to think it and one day they
tell us about flowers or children they have grown,
or causes they love. Billions of thin streaks

of light flow. Permeable membranes flash,
letting ions in and letting ions out, quick
as lightning, an electrostatic charge, running.

Inside our cells, we each add wax to wax.
In the darkness at 5 am, a square of light comes on.
Over the rim of the planet, a friend has just had lunch. ⁄⁄

Amina Alyal

Space Bubble

That was the time of the great insulation,
a staycation in an inside-out home, not home,
sealed off like a space station, no egress
except in a hazmat suit, no escape
from our own atmosphere. There was nothing

to do except read poetry, and no need to look
at anything except each mark on the wall
and all the news from Mars. Earth emerged
as a unified, elderly globe in slow motion,
one haphazard heap of a discount store
no one could pay for. In space,

they photographed astronauts' eyes to see
if the lack of gravity makes them any lighter
than the long hair rising above our heads.
But we in our cells bared our teeth
and snarled at the strangers shackling our ankles,
not looking as they wept at a single pure drop of rain.

Today, as dark glass blocks out what used to be shops,
sun shines. Folk show their faces to all and sundry.
A cosmonaut reads out a poem
over steely white lakes in a slate-blue scape.
Earth turns again, and we're all coming home. ⫽

Three Dante Poems

Inferno: Ghosts in the Machine

We have learned how to shrink to the tiniest image, big as
a bee in a tight box, and then to swell as large as
billboards. We/they have left our flesh behind, and demons
grin and growl all over the hurtbox, grinding away the last
autonomous neuron. We finger material, running our
fingers over the hems, and call out, *Don't forget us,*
remembering how we used to live without avatars, but how
now the best kind of fight will always be over whether
snow is fire, and this will rage without end. *Don't forget us
don't get us do for us doofus don't make a fuss.* Head swaps
are easy, letters typing themselves out, which is freedom.
Yesterday my head was as sleek as Anubis, today I can
flaunt a chimera. *Anubis a newbie an anus the bis that's
the bis it's a buzz.* All the birds bleed from the loss of their
wings. I can't be bothered with material, and only weep
when pixels die and suffer, while ghosts are the ones to tell
us what we used to know when we listen to them on the
phone. Ghosts cancel each other out and threads of
electricity are fiercer than the noose. We dread a Report
that proves we don't exist, as language crumbles and
aimbots poke all our politicians into pits of sewage and fire.
We pull the real cloth over our knees but we no longer feel
the threads when they slip all over the floor.

Purgatorio: On the Verge

We have sewn our own eyes shut, so we don't see the bags
of provisions going over the edge. Hordes of us lie,
bereave(d of move)ment. We/they lie in half-lit rows of beds
– too dim to walk any more – calling out, *Is this Hell?*
Burdened, we climb the tiers. The giant sloth emboldens us
to run, bearing leaden tons of gravity, away from the rising
graphs, the ups and downs, the flat, flat lines. Rats come
out of the woodwork but they don't carry plague, just the
hope of a cleaner planet. So we race, staying in place, like
the Red Queen, in this backwards game of bones. Weeping

Amina Alyal

floods the streets, makes it dangerous to pass; half the roads are closed, the other half deserted. It's like house arrest, we/they say. It's lockdown. It's locking ourselves in with stitches we have applied ourselves, so we don't see the bags of fertiliser thrown over the edge. We don't want our bodies morphed by way of experiment, the way they do it in Hell. We don't want to eat morphed grain. We would rather starve, we/they say. But the ones that don't say, just starve. Who is left to farm when all of us are lying, heavy with boulders, our eyes sewn shut with our own needles, pecking up grain and adding it to the hoards we cover with our own bodies, climbing the tears? Angels appear and we clap them but we/they don't pay for the service.

Paradiso: Reeds

You arrive at the stars, which can only be seen because they are dead. Last night you were playing the piano and now it's the harmony that makes your words fade like snow as you grasp at the fifths and sixths, measure the length of a note in a hard piece of reed, which is the same as the stem curving into a circular hoop where threads cross in squares, crossed again by stitches and it's the other side you want to see, although you find when you look that all of space has shrunk to a dot. That's when you are at your best, when the planets align and you can see all the way along a line of stars and see that you are here as well as there at the same time. There are angels on your hearthstone, but always too large, or too small, for life. They say very little but angels like animals don't need to speak. Speech is for those who can't communicate. Your voice tells you to be mindful, and you tell yourself that Socrates was a scientist when he said not knowing was all you need. You sharpen a reed pen with a scalpel blade and the ink runs into melting drifts. You float on a rock amongst plasma swells and surges, a pebble of a rock that just contains your soft haunches, and this isn't a parallel universe although you do know they exist. //

Angela Reid

Angela Reid has taught English to teenage girls, sailed the high seas on tall ships and hiked in Vietnam, Nepal and along many National trails in England. She began writing ten years ago and has almost completed her memoir. Her writing explores her interests in her family, gardening, travel and the sea.

A Golden Bowl

Let me consider how I spent my time
in lockdown, when confined to home:
I tried to write, and sometimes turned to rhyme,
but failed with that and struggled all alone.
And so I joined an online writing class
and met, with joy, a great creative group:
some shy, some brave, some bold as molten brass —
oh, this was better! Can I stay in the loop?
And so we all wrote haiku in the rain,
found joy in Nature, sorrow in the soul,
watched birds, discovered all that buried pain,
and poured our words into a golden bowl.
'Twas worth it, all the endless trials of Zoom,
to be included in the Writing Room. //

May Evening

In the early evening sunlight
I stand
beneath the maples' acrid yellow flowers
to gaze
along a purple bluebell haze
past silver-barked statues
towards the startling beech green beyond.

Light shines through transparent freshness.
Pollen flicks the air.
A blackbird pierces the evening.

This moment will not last.

Leaves will coarsen,
blossoms fade,
colours change.

Autumn fruits –
the golden quince,
the rosy apple –
attempt a consolation.

Cobwebs glisten
as they clothe the hedges,
bonfires smoke and smoulder,
frost sugars the grass.

Beyond skeletal oaks
the blood-red sun of winter solstice

reverses. //

Angela Reid

Lines

Washing lines link me to the past,
tie to drudgery or delightful domesticity,
tether to family.

The first, a cheap blue plastic cord,
hooked tree to tree across a patch of grass
– the middle held aloft
by nobbled Y-topped stick –
where loops of terry-towelling nappies
flapped freely
and empty baby-grows
took tentative unsupported steps.

With time, it filled each day
with little skirts, small dresses, pink leotards
and party frocks – all frills and sashes –
until jeans and tight T shirts slouched across,
announcing independence.

Then empty.

Empty.

Discarded then the thin cord,
replaced by revolutionary rotation
suitable for office shirts
empty of cufflinks
– arms waving
and drowning.

Shoulder pegged to shoulder for support,
they link to ink-stained blouses,
proof of serious endeavours.
Outer garments conceal neglected knickers,
sagging boxer shorts
and socks and socks and socks.

Angela Reid   22

Now, when I peg flapping flags of pillowcases
and billowing double sheets,
like pristine sails or shrouds,
lines envelop me,
wrap me in memories,
to free me to the wind and sun. //

Angela Reid

Oceans of Memory

On a bleached shingle beach
in Cefalonia
these are the tides of Odysseus

still here
still there.

Waves collapse
hushed
and suck through glistening pebbles

again
again.

Salt crystals
sparkle in sunshine,
dry on stones
like crystal memories of sun-baked days.

Decades later under blue Caribbean skies
at the edge of another island
the Atlantic crashes
on rocks pitted by the spray of aeons.

Thunderous invasions explode
in deep caverns
while on a half-moon sheltered bay
waves chase synchronised sandpipers
or scuttling crabs
and leave foam-frothed seaweed treasures
scattered on an empty beach.

On another edge of the ocean
a cold grey sea rolls in
all swelling energy released
as waves fold

pause

crash.

Icy east winds whip off the sea
to scrape the skin
with swirling sand.

In my dreams
all seas gather in one great tsunami
abandoning earth
to spiral round Poseidon,
weave through Orion's Belt
and girdle the moon. ⌁

Angela Reid

Surviving the Storm

'She's a survivor all right,' announced my sister through gritted teeth.

I tried to picture my mother, ninety-one years old and back in hospital.

There is something admirable about the way in which, defying all good sense and reason, she insists on living alone in Smeaton Cottage: a four-storey granite house built into Cornish rock facing the Atlantic.

I thought about last year's chest infection, and then a broken hip, and the time when she was allowed out of a care home for a brief visit. Reunited with her views of the sea, the lighthouse beyond and the wheeling seagulls above, she turned her sorrowful eyes to me, her face gaunt with pain.

'Don't put me in a home permanently, darling. I would rather die. When the time comes, just open the bedroom window and tip me out on a Spring tide.'

Be careful what you wish for.

On February 1st, 2014, Mary had been standing in her kitchen, a former pilchard cellar, stirring a pan of homemade lactose and gluten-free delights – no frozen food or meals on wheels for her! No doubt her excitement was rising like the tide outside her window.

The storms which had been battering the South Coast for ten days had changed direction. The high tide and fifty-mile-an-hour gale were now driving directly from the East and hurtling towards her granite walls.

I imagine the rocks rumbling and the waves lashing against the kitchen window may have given her slight concern, but she will have consoled herself with the thought that the house had withstood storms for well over two hundred years. She'd had a new window with reinforced glass put in only last year. Nevertheless, the noise must have been disconcerting.

Maybe this was the moment she decided to phone me.

'Listen to this, darling.' She would have been holding the phone towards the window.

On the answerphone I heard howling wind, grinding boulders, the splash and scatter of sea and stones as they battered the window and Radio 4 murmuring in the background.

'It's high tide in about half an hour,' she informed me before signing off.

Only later did I learn how, with sudden devastating force, at the height of the tide and storm, the whole window, including frame, burst in from its precarious socket, followed by half a ton of ice cold Atlantic, full of sand, stones and gravel. And then another wave, and another. No time for Canute instructions here.

Dashed to the tiled floor, she gashed her head and floundered in the swirling waters. Unable to stagger to her feet, she scrabbled about trying to grasp something stable as the water flooded in, wave after wave.

But she survived. Angels must have been watching over her.

Two minutes before, her solicitor and his wife, on a visit to their weekend cottage, had popped in to watch the storm of the century from her upstairs windows. The view would have been spectacular.

Still standing with their coats on as the window, unbroken, crashed in, they held on to the sturdy pine table as the water engulfed them too. But they acted quickly, pulling Mary out of a potential watery end.

Drenched, shocked and bleeding as she was, her first and only words were, 'Charles, turn the electricity off NOW!'

More angels followed. Her neighbour, usually wary of my mother's demands, opened her door on this occasion. Her granddaughter was there: a trainee paramedic. While waiting for the ambulance, she dealt with shock and hypothermia, found a change of clothes, and took all the details necessary so my mother could be admitted to hospital without delay.

27   Angela Reid

Half an hour later, Mary insisted on walking up the slight hill to the ambulance, delayed because of the flooding, issuing instructions to the firemen who were battling to put the window back, and pumping the water out of the ground floor.

Yes, she is a survivor. Undefeated by life's challenges and a full array of physical ailments, she rises again, a fragile, grey-haired phoenix. My mother. ⁄⁄

Bebe Stables

Conceived in India and possessed by a storyteller genie. Raised in Africa. Matured in Britain and America. Adulterated in Europe. Recently, my genie nudged me: 'Let's dish out our tales between a curry cookbook, three novels, two plays and a musical.' More? My genie is stirring...

Acknowledgements:
'The Perfect Dinner or How News Travels' after 'The Bohemian Dinner' by Charles Green Shaw.

Rainy Day Haiku

I
Leave home with no word!
Float off to the autumn dance!
Grounded! For ever!

II
That red winter cape
is thrown to the ground for you.
Maple's chivalry.

III
Oaks stand shivering.
They reach for grey kaftan folds.
Earth stole their gold robes.

IV
Charcoal branches write
runes on winter's slate of sky;
a crow's nest full stop.

V
Curl wet leaves round your
fingertips and play a pipe.
Nymph, dance in the rain! ⁄⁄

Things Change

stood high
our statues
for heroes but
now we read them differently

then sky larks
singers of fables
conceived them
to burnish our shine

homage to strength
mettle and sweat
furnaced and cast
into great moulds

now it's the crow's *kraa*
patina dulled
our statues
are levelled ⁄⁄

Bebe Stables

The Perfect Dinner or How News Travels

A carpeted corridor – The wide staircase – Then the marble reception

A haughty maître d' – The walk to the window – Then a white damask cloth

A keen young waiter – The leather-bound menu – Then warm bread rolls

An earnest sommelier – The Merlot poured – Then fulsome fruit taste

An order taken – The anticipation – Then silver domes

A dramatic revelation – The herbal aroma – Then comforting flavours

A total satisfaction – The perfect dinner – Then an observation…

A wonderful meal but … – …The perfect isn't memorable!– Then we laugh!

A dessert arrives – The Tarte au Citron sun – Then orbited by drizzled coulis

A bizarre taste? – The strangeness of mustard! – Then the waiter called

A gentle complaint made – The red-faced waiter – Then desserts removed

An explanation – *The mustard dressing…* – Then, *…was in the dessert fridge.*

A mango coulis… – …the identical colour… – Then, *…so easily switched!*

A new dessert arrives – The coulis is true mango – Then all is well

A final coffee – The walk up to bed – Then oblivion

A carpeted corridor – The wide staircase – Then the marble reception

A fresh new waiter – The morning greeting – Then to the table

A clean white table cloth – The breakfast menu – Then the order made

A waiter's amiable grin – The wink – Then, *Any **mustard** with your Full English?* ⁄⁄

Greedy

All I wanted for Christmas was a lovely house in the woods. We had gone over to Cirencester to check my little holiday-let cottage and add Christmas decorations ready for the December guests. We always look at properties for sale when we are over there. I suppose it's the feeling that one day the toing and froing between North London and Cirencester will get too much and that it might be an idea to move back to the place where we still have many friends. It may seem as though I'm a bit of a goose, but there is no harm in thinking about possibilities is there?

My habitual wishful thinking usually involves looking at books on Amazon. But visits to Cirencester change my browsing habits to Zoopla and Rightmove. For example, I'd noticed that since March there has been a truly wonderful property listed which – unlike my holiday-let cottage – would not fit into a Christmas stocking! It is a gloriously long, organic, curving house, with five bedrooms, standing on stilts in seven acres of woodland. And the biggest surprise is the price. We could sell our modest house in Hertfordshire, buy this and have a decent amount of change to spare. The fact it has not yet sold is like being presented with a menu for a Christmas dinner with stuffing and all the trimmings.

I let my mind conjure that long winding organic home in the woodland. I picture seven or eight shepherd's huts or log cabins hidden among the acres of trees to create a writer's retreat. I watch myself sellotape an invitation on every door, 'You're invited to sherry at the big house at 6pm.' In the early evenings, our guests share the best part of their writing day, or their writer's block and cures for it, or tips for fuelling our brief flames of creativity. We enjoy each other's company until we separate again for more writing, dinner or a round or two at the Wild Duck next door. I really want that house. I'm hungry for it. Yet there's apprehension too; maybe my dreams are way bigger than my energy these days. Maybe I'm being greedy.

I mention it to my husband Robert. 'I'd buy it,' I say wistfully.

Bebe Stables

'The trouble is,' he says, 'there's not a single Santa's elf that can magic it into existence.'

'What do you mean?'

'It's an architect's 3-D mock-up.' And he should know – he's an architect.

The house on Zoopla is displayed like any real house that someone wanted to sell. There is the picture of the outside of the building. It sits convincingly in a clearing, surrounded by tall trees. Then the usual room views, some taken from different directions so that you could get a feeling for size. The choice of furnishings is modern and mellow. There are even pictures on the walls. It all looks so tactile – but these are all just highly convincing visuals.

'That's crackers! They've made it look so real! Why would anyone do that?'

'To show what can be done with the site,' he says.

It strikes me that there should be a covenant with the land that only allows people with imagination to buy it. My worry is that a developer is going to snap it up, fell all the trees and fill the site with the flat facades of soulless boxes.

I sigh.

I'm inviting world-famous authors and internationally renowned writing gurus to run workshops. They arrive from all corners of the globe. They compliment me on the circular guest suite, clean and crisp as an honesty seed pod. After a productive day, they sink into the deep mattress, lulled by the spirit of the woodland around them and the blessings of trees.

It's all just a dream. And dreams have no calories or cost. I realise there's an important reality inside a dream: it's the place where you can be as greedy as you like! /

Carole Burgess

Carole Burgess sailed small boats as a teenager, tried ballet in her twenties and now practices yoga and meditation. She has lived in KwaZulu and Sri Lanka, and has managed organisations seeking justice and peace. Her poems are inspired by colour, texture and memory. Carole lives in Chester.

Through my Skin

The curfew is announced as we eat
cheese omelettes in the Elephant Café.
Soldiers, slung with guns, pool out of vans
on the street outside. Deep shadow,
machine gun movement stuttering like a cine film –
we stand. Plates fall, staccato,
a sudden hailstorm on a tin roof.

On the bus we're jammed in, tense and prickly heat.
Minor explosions detonate as feet clamber,
clatter on the roof, and legs, bags, chickens
flail against the window. The smell
of heat on cloth, on dark, glistening skin.
Pressed into a stranger's back I take in
language: Tamil, Sinhalese, terror.

My last day, on the roof terrace,
you do that thing Sri Lankan men do –
untie the lungi around your waist,
waft for air then fold in,
re-budding a rose.
Up close against your chest
I take in language through my skin. ⁄⁄

Carole Burgess   40

Valentine

Ox heart, sliced, on my plate.
Smooth velvety flesh, close-textured
like pink pressed powder, a blueish tinge.
Three of us sit at the Formica breakfast bar,
sixties kitchen straw yellow,
like living in a beehive.
Black Start-Rite sandals, white socks,
on the wooden footrest, feet poised
for flight, to find the future.

Donegal hostel, lying low at the field's edge.
Mould makes a Rothko abstract, green on green,
curtains caught by pegs and orange trailer twine.
Jesus and Mary, his 'n' hers in matching frames
present their hearts, vermilion, pulsating pop pics
blazoned on merchandise.
Across the window a white bird rises,
shears the world in two.
Here, wood scrapes on tile, a door opens. ✍

Carole Burgess

Watch

We circle the curving bay slowly,
walk in step; pause
to look at the view.

Limpid shallows, charcoal line of coast draws the gaze to
Moel-y-Gest rising, humpbacked on the horizon
like a whale stranded,
beached.

We turn for the marina,
follow the inlet to the harbour,
a forest of masts close moored,
tethered.

Outside the clubhouse, industrial size
washing machines squat, ready for the detritus of sailors
as they prepare to make way and
cast off.

Foam churns against the porthole
like a tiller cranked into life.
On the forenoon watch
the mariner waits

for the tide to turn,
for the wind to freshen,
and the sail to fill, like scudding clouds across the sky,

and the whole world and its secrets lie open
as a clean sheet thrown across a bed. //

Playground

green grass blue paint peeling on the slide
like a dockside crane towering

far away swings with their threat of heavy chain
rushing tarmac where silent teenagers grapple

your orange Chopper cast on its side
will you go out with me

I look up into the sun study your forehead cheekbone
chin
then the soft yellow cotton of my pleated skirt

and the quick path home breathless ⁄⁄

Carole Burgess

Deborah Ripley

Deborah Ripley is a freelance graphic designer and photographer, working in the creative industries for several decades. She splits her time between London and Hastings in Sussex. She has only recently taken up writing and is enjoying the new possibilities it presents.

Shadows on the Lawn

I was a daygirl at the local convent, not out of religious affiliation but lack of local school choice. Wednesday afternoons were art class, which I liked. We had a grand classroom with a vaulted high ceiling. Twenty-four nine- and ten-year-old girls sat at wooden desks.

'Put your overalls on and come and get your paints and paper,' ordered Mrs Kemp. I pulled my blue, paint-stained tabard over my head and tied neat bows at the sides.

Chair legs scraped and screeched against the wooden floor as we rushed to the huge plan-chest next to her desk. Large round tablets of cheap bright paint sat in white plastic palettes; a pile of unrefined paper next to them. Bedraggled paintbrushes. Dirty jam jars. A cluster of girls, pushing against one another, stretching and grabbing for the cleanest palettes, the newest paints.

Back at my desk, I was aware Janet was sitting somewhere behind me. Perhaps she was taking one of my felt pens out of my pencil case. I shot a glance at her as I walked to the small ante-room at the back of the class to fill my jam jar, but she didn't look up. I felt uneasy.

A few weeks earlier, my parents had collected Janet from the Convent so we could spend Sunday together. We were in the same class and we'd recently become friends, me a day-girl and she a boarder. After lunch, Mum and Dad drove us to a local garden for the afternoon and Janet and I wandered off, a little bored, amongst the huge rhododendrons and spicy, fragrant azalea trees that so captivated my parents. The early summer sun saturated the blooms. Large, inky shadows soaking the lawns.

At school the following week, I noticed my pencil case was missing. I glanced around the classroom and spotted it on Janet's desk.

'Why have you got my pencil case?'

'It needed liberating,' she said coolly. 'I'm keeping it for a while. I'll give it back when I'm ready.'

Halfway through class, I went to change the water in my jam jar. When I got back to my desk, a sheet of art paper had appeared on top of my half-finished work. 'I'm going to take all your friends,' scrawled in blood-red paint against a scrubby background of I don't know what.

At first I thought it might be from Janet, although she wasn't popular so I couldn't be sure. I scanned the room nervously, girls concentrated on their work, heads down, the tinkling sound of paintbrushes on glass.

Rosemary was looking directly at me from the other side of the room. Rosemary, blond, red-faced and podgy. It was her. Looking down at the red warning I wondered what I had done, which friends she meant? All of them, it said. Perhaps everyone in class. That was a lot of girls. I felt light-headed and nauseous, floating without an anchor.

Instinctively I folded the message so nobody else would see it and pushed it down in the waste paper bin. Smudging the words, I had red paint on my hands and I washed them in the ante-room in ice-cold water that belched and bubbled from the tarnished brass tap, swirling scarlet into the plug hole. The final bell of the day rang and we cleared up.

In the car on the way home, I told my mother Rosemary had said she was taking all my friends in a red paint message.

'Do you know where she lives?' she asked me.

'Yes,' I said.

We drove to the estate, to the road, to her house. A neat and modern sixties build. Trimmed apple-green grass on each side of the path to the front door. Very different to our magical bungalow in the woods. From the back seat of the Hillman Minx, I watched my mother walk up the path and ring the doorbell. I kept the car windows shut. Mrs White opened the door and they appeared to be speaking. I think it was for less than three minutes and then Mum was back in the car and we were on our way home.

The next day I waited nervously for the repercussions that never came. One uneventful lesson followed another, flowing into the days and weeks that led to the end of term.

Mrs Kemp shouted orders as usual. My pencil case had gone forever.

Liberated from dread by the summer holidays, I lay around in our huge back garden, a woodland-boundaried paradise. Prone on a sun lounger and warmed by August sun I would close my eyes and listen to the soft hissing of the pressure spray as Dad drowned unwanted dandelions in weedkiller, clip-clip-clipping as Mum trimmed the roses with secateurs and the thud of the dog collapsing as close to my sun lounger as he could, panting in the heat. ⁄⁄

The Caravan

My childhood home was an elongated bungalow on a lawn in the centre of a cradle of woodland. It was set back from the lane by a long driveway. Each dwelling on the lane was as different as its owner and most were hidden from the track by trees and undergrowth. Mysterious spinster sisters lived opposite in a gloomy red brick house shrouded by giant oaks. A few hundred yards further, a brash man and his vicious dog lived in his self-built dream home with a swimming pool. Next door to him were naturists that ran a cattery.

Our immediate neighbours were our friends Angie and Rob. Mum and I went for elevenses with Angie two or three times a week in my school holidays. We trampled a path through the shared hedge of nettles and barbed brambles, getting scratched or stung.

Rob was six foot six, a lanky Jim Reeves devotee in a white shirt, blue jeans and big black boots. His dark hair was prematurely thinning. A car mechanic, Rob had hands permanently stained with Duckham's gear oil. Rob kept other rusty industrial items in his shed including a tractor. After work and at weekends, he'd ride it up into the woods alongside our garden boundary and I would glimpse him through the hedge, high up and mighty in his metal seat, rifle across his lap. He was setting or checking the traps he'd set for foxes – cruel, rusty metal-toothed contraptions waiting to snap shut. To his disappointment, he mostly snared timid, soft beige rabbits who were then ravaged by the foxes he had hoped to catch.

I remember him showing us his latest acquisition one afternoon, a chick hatchery. There were glass-fronted wooden drawers full of eggs, some cracking open, revealing matted yellow feathery down inside. I longed to see a proper chick, like on my Easter cards, but I never did.

'They'll all die,' Mum said. 'He doesn't know what he's doing.'

Rob's wife Angie was a hairdresser and had luxurious curls, dyed pitch black. She wore black eyeliner with small flicks at the outer edges and winged cat-eye glasses. She was small-town stylish in her bright red coat and pointed stilettos. Mum and I would sit in the kitchen of their dilapidated home and drink instant coffee (Mum) or fizzy orange (me). I loved these visits, especially after their baby, Louise was born because I was allowed to hold her. I could smell baby powder mixed with cabbage and mince. Mum said they were 'common'. Less of a slight, more of a context.

Rob had promised to build Angie a proper house so after Louise was born it was time to knock down the shack and make a start. They moved into a grubby caravan next to the shed. The caravan was small and difficult with a new baby and a tall, gangly husband and the house build was slow. Mum and I would squeeze into the tiny kitchen space for our coffee and orange. I liked it and pretended we were in a doll's house. In summer we all sat outside in the heat on half-broken deckchairs, Angie perched on the caravan steps and Louise crawling on the unkempt grass. Friends often ambled up their driveway and we'd get into conversation. Sometimes a handsome man called Danny would appear. I thought he looked like a cowboy in a Western film, tall and sunburned brown. Once after he'd gone and it was just the three of us, Angie said she was fed up with the caravan and fed up with Rob. She was looking straight at Mum when she said it. Mum didn't say anything.

One Saturday afternoon our phone rang and Mum answered. It was Rob. I was sitting on the sofa and I could hear his tiny voice coming from the green plastic handset even though it was close to Mum's ear.

'Angie's gone,' he screamed. 'She's been at it with Danny.'

Mum was good in a crisis. 'Where is she, Rob?' she asked him.

'I don't bloody know. Danny's gone off in his car. He's got his shotgun. Says he's going to blow his head off if Angie stops seeing him.'

Mum knew more than she let on. She picked up the car keys.

'Can I come?' I asked her. 'Yes,' she said, 'but you'll stay in the car.'

There were two or three caravans side by side just visible from Hayhurst Hill as you came round the bend. Damp, lichen-covered breeze blocks. The windows were grey, opaque nothing. Angie was in one of these dank boxes. Mum got out of the car and crossed the road, walked up the muddy driveway and disappeared into the gloom. Ten minutes later she was back and we went home.

'She's in a terrible state,' she said to Dad when we got back. 'Silly girl.'

Later on, Mum spoke to Danny on the phone. The door to the sitting room was shut and I couldn't make out what was being said. She was quite a long time. Dad was in the veg garden pulling up potatoes for supper.

Angie stayed in the breezeblock caravan with baby Louise until things settled down. Mum and I went to visit a couple of times but I didn't really like it there.

Rob worked on the new house every evening and weekend. Angie and Louise came home and they were all moved in by Christmas. A year later, Gary was born. Mum and I went through the hedge again and Angie played Elvis records for us in the new living room. It was loud but it didn't wake the kids. Mum was right; none of the chicks survived. I don't think Danny killed himself but I don't remember ever seeing him again. //

I am a Block of Flats

I am a block of flats.
It was not always so.
My rooms have seen
business of several kinds.
I have a guestbook, somewhere.

I am tall, I see for miles
to Beachy Head, to Primark.
My skin is dry and cracked
eyes watering inwardly, salty tears
drenching my carpets.

My entrance is shabby,
tubules of ash flake casually
on my stairs,
stale stinks
betray a hidden canker.

I am a block of flats
wearing a mossy green garland
and rusty stripes, hoping
I am beautiful enough
to catch an eye,
to be loved again. ⁄⁄

Superfood

George

We were at Sliced and I thought if I tried something different, Sally would be pleased. So I did. I had a prawn and avocado sandwich on granary bread. I wasn't sure at first. Slimy, I thought. I hoped Sally didn't see me make a face. I'm as happy with cheese and pickle. Branston and some medium-cut cheddar. I like white sliced farmhouse but Sally says there's no nutritional value in it. I could easily eat a cheese and pickle sandwich with a tea every day. I never get tired of them.

Sally's eyes were on me, waiting for me to say I didn't like the sandwich. She had salad in a cardboard box. I think it was called superfood, but it looked like leaves and small acorns. Made me think of autumn in the woods. Not something I'd eat. Anyway, I was trying to make her think I was enjoying my sandwich. I hadn't seen her for six weeks and I didn't want to annoy her.

Sally

I was over the moon he suggested going to Sliced. We usually go to the Pergola. He always has cheese and pickle on white and I have prawn and avocado on brown. He has tea and I have a sparkling water (which he doesn't see the point of). In the queue, I always say, 'White bread is basically empty carbohydrates. Just sugar really.' 'That's interesting,' he says. Then he orders his sandwich on white. Jesus Christ, I think.

There's not much to talk about because he doesn't do anything except the crossword. We have nothing in common. And now he's retired and Mum's gone, it's like pulling teeth. I try to introduce new ideas, like last time when we were talking – or at least I was talking – about nutrition and looking after your health. And I think, Dad, pick me up on something, ask me something. But no. He listens patiently

Deborah Ripley

but gives nothing back. I know I shouldn't complain. He could be a horrible old man.

George

Me and Doreen used to go to the Pergola every Saturday for lunch and we always had the same thing. I'd have steak and kidney pie with mash and peas and Doreen loved fish and chips. We knew what we liked and that was that. Now I'm retired, I go to the Pergola for lunch every day. Enzo brings my sandwich and tea over as soon as I've taken my coat off and put my paper on the table. Even on Saturdays. Anyway, we went up to the counter because Sally wanted to see what they had. 'Have you got sourdough?' she said. I wasn't sure what that was so I kept quiet. 'Just sliced brown or white darlin',' Enzo said and I think he winked at me which made me nervous in case she saw. She went for brown, with prawns and avocado. 'No mayo or butter,' she said. 'No problem, love,' said Enzo.

A few days later I passed Sliced. I thought they were still building it because it was all scaffolding and planks. But people were sitting down eating and the planks were tables. A bit rough and ready but different. When Sally rang I suggested it and she said, 'Oh great, let's go there!' and I was relieved I'd come up with a good idea.

Sally

Sliced! Amazing. When we sat down I asked him if he'd had prawns or avocado before. I knew he'd say no. He said there was a prawn and avocado starter at the works Christmas dinner one year. But he and Mum hadn't liked the look of it so they went for the tomato soup. 'It's really easy to make fresh tomato soup at home,' I said, 'it's really good for you and doesn't have all the additives. I can show you how to make it.' 'That would be nice,' he said.

At home, I sat on the sofa and stared into space. Then I cried. I love him so much and he's tried so hard. But he's infuriating. When he got the diagnosis, I searched online for anything I could find that might help. I told him a better diet with less additives and sugar and carbs could help. But it doesn't seem to land. I love him and I hate him. It's torture.

George

When we said goodbye, she said she'd come over again in a couple of weeks. Normally it's a month between visits. I hope she doesn't feel sorry for me. When I knocked the tea over at Sliced I was cross with myself. I can usually manage without using my right hand, then nobody sees the shakes. I've got in the habit of keeping it under the table. But Sally said, 'Pass me a napkin,' and I wasn't thinking. 'Dad!' she shouted. It went everywhere and the mug smashed to bits on the concrete floor. When I got home I noticed drops of tea all over my trousers.

Sally rang at the weekend, a lovely surprise. She said she'd come to the house, so I've been cleaning and tidying. I keep the house up to scratch. Doreen was houseproud and it's stuck with me. I always wash up directly after I've eaten. And I put Toilet Duck round the rim every night before bed just after I've cleaned my teeth.

I thought I'd get some lunch in. I could get prawns and avocado. I could make us some sandwiches earlier on and cover them with clingfilm. That's what Doreen always did. I'd better write it down just in case I forget. Writing's difficult now with my shaky hand. I'll get some apples as well, she's always pestering me to eat more fruit. She said she was going to bring some tomatoes with her so she could show me how to make tomato soup from scratch. I'm not sure I'm all that keen but I'll show willing. It's a lot of bother when I'm perfectly happy with a tin of Heinz. //

Deborah Ripley

My Mother is a Care Home

my mother is a care home
she glides through rooms
each one a trove
an invisible library
of autobiographies

in silence
guests sift memories
carefully
gazing through windows
storing or discarding

my mother is a care home
she glides through rooms
recently vacated
delighting in dust that
twinkles in shards of sunlight ⁄⁄

Elke Heckel

Elke Heckel was born in rural Germany and has spent most of her adult life in London. She is a retired midwife and moved with her partner to Ramsgate in 2019 where she enjoys sea swimming. Prior to joining the Words from a Distance workshops she wrote travel journals and co-translated poetry.

Nature's Throne

My lover leads the way through the broken wall, ignoring the 'keep out' signs. It's the eighties and it is still the time of squats and wild neglected urban spaces.

'This is my special place,' he tells me. A secret garden now, where once they cleaned London's drinking water and put an end to cholera. It is overgrown – giant hogweed reaches up into the grey sky, and brambles claw at my dungarees as he helps me across a wall. I breathe in deeply. The honey scent of buddleia and the unmistakable aroma of fig are such a welcome contrast to the fumes on the busy Leabridge Road which we crossed to get here. Soon I see a giant fig tree leaning down towards the river where water rushes through the weir. The water smells like the grey cloying mud you find on the bottom of ponds. Mysterious relics of metal machinery and tracks poke out between the undergrowth. I am relieved that the stench of the past is long gone.

Five years on, we take our son and his friends. There are two gates now with opening times and information boards and there is art! Nature has been tamed.

'Nature's throne' is our son's favourite place – the kids run ahead squealing with excitement; they love playing hide and seek by the sculpture. Huge granite blocks placed in a circle, dug up from the original works, some with round spy holes where once pipes cut through. In the centre stands the biggest one, carved with Celtic symbols, it looks like a gigantic throne.

The seeker has to lean against its back: 'One, two, three ... twenty! Coming to find you – ready or not!'

If you touch the throne before you get caught you won't be 'it' next time. In the end they all get lifted up onto the throne.

'I am the king of the castle!'

'No I am!'

'I am!!!!!'

Yet I miss the wildness of the past.

The children skip down the path and balance on the tracks. Around and above us trees have taken over the filter beds and a choir of birds greets us. We step onto the mysterious moss-covered stone dial and lie down on our backs holding hands. The children stop wriggling, quietly listening to the sound of a nearby woodpecker. Before we leave they spy the fish peeping out between the reeds in the filter beds next to the exit.

That's the other artwork, 'Rise and shine', glazed oversized ceramic fish, iridescent in the sunshine, rising from the water. Grudgingly I admit that it might be better than before but Peter won't hear of it.

'Gentrification, nowhere wild, nowhere to discover, nowhere to hide,' he grumbles. A sentiment that was set to repeat itself with him for the next two decades – glorifying the past, resenting the present and fearing the future.

Twenty-five years later I hold my new lover's hand: 'Let me show you a special place.' I tell him about the fish – sadly long smashed – now only their pedestals visible in the dried up reed beds, next to the board with the artist's description of what once was. The walls are covered in graffiti and a new community of city dwellers are living just outside on their barges. I cover his eyes and lead him to the throne. He places his hands on the cool granite, his fingers tracing the carving. He opens his eyes and smiles at me. A smile full of affection and appreciation. He climbs up first and pulls me up next to him. We sit cross-legged, knees touching, fingers intertwined, looking down the track towards the mysterious emerald, moss-covered dial – both grateful for new beginnings. //

Elke Heckel

My Robe

I want a beautiful robe
made of silk
not too heavy
not too flimsy
just right
both warm and cool to the touch
changing colour in the light like the sea

thunderous greys
shimmering turquoises
deep greens
silver threads sparkling
like the sun reflecting off the waves

I want to pull it round me like a cocoon
curling up

When I take it out its wide sleeves inflate in the wind like wings
I run along the sea shore, feeling the firm sand under my feet
shouting at

the sea
        the sky
                the world

until I reach the water's edge
I drop it there

a sharp in-breath and a yelp as I meet the first wave
soon the water caresses me
angst, fear and fury are left at the shore
and invigorating joy embraces me as I ride the waves ⫽

Elke Heckel   64

Kahili Ginger
(Hedychium gardnerianum)

I smell you before I see you. You are blooming like never before.

Your flamboyant flower spikes are made up of many slender primrose yellow sepals and petals pierced by long flaming orange-red stamens. Descended from the Himalayas you have been taken all over the world by plant collectors. In Hawaii your sisters have become invaders, their seeds spread by birds.

A friend grew you from seed many years ago. In my London garden you survived several winters outdoors, against the odds, your tubers turned to slush by frost.

Surely I have killed you through neglect, I thought guiltily more than once.

But then just as I made plans to move another into your terracotta pot, you poked a green finger up at me. A green, pointy shoot that quickly grew into a strong, exotic, juicy green frond soon joined by others, your threatened demise a distant memory.

There were some years when we managed to bring you in before the frost. This left you thirsty, twisting for the light, half dead and only springing back to life outdoors. You discarded the dry husks of last year's growth until your green, pointy fingers emerged in quick succession once again.

You are tough and forgiving and I am glad of it. Why have you blossomed so profusely now? Not a swan song, I hope. The sea air? Enhanced pandemic attention? For once you have emerged from winter looking perfect. We put you out on the terrace and feast our eyes on you during alfresco pandemic breakfasts.

'Isn't she looking healthy? I think she likes it here!'

But then come high winds from the North East. While we retreat indoors you stay out and sure enough turn yellow, and your leaves frizzle. They call it windburn here. I cut your fronds one by one, berating myself for my impatience.

Elke Heckel

'There was no frost, you know!' I tell you, but still I feel your silent reproach.

Before long, green finger shoots emerge once more and not just that, your leaves grow flower buds. Just before they are ready to burst open in late autumn we bring you in – both for your protection and our delectation.

What a delight and comfort you are, your beauty and exotic scent invoking holidays in Thailand, Malaysia, India, Zimbabwe – and yet even a trip to the green houses of Kew is out of our reach. You inspire scented mind travel during the pandemic lockdown.

Is it too greedy to hope for seed pods as pretty as flowers? Seed capsules splitting into orange segments revealing fleshy red seeds: a flaming second display. I use a soft brush to imitate a pollinator. Can I be trusted to grow your babies? How I would love to share you with friends old and new. I water and feed you to show you just how much I care; in response you drool down on me. Cool rivulets find their way from leafy tips down my spine and make me shiver as I write this. ⁄⁄

Bruno

She is woken by the howling wind and the glare of the sunrise streaming through the bedroom window. It is breathtaking, swirls of purple rising above layers of orange, pink and turquoise – in the far distance she can glimpse the sea, glistening in coppers and golds. The wind comes off the sea and is strong – so strong the gulls are flying backwards.

A month ago this would have filled her with delight, she would have snuggled up to Bruno, stroked his belly and told him, 'Wake up, just a little, just one eye, look! Isn't it beautiful!'

He would have groaned and opened one eye, smiling at her first and then at the scene outside.

'Aren't we lucky.'

Both bathed in golden light, they would have wrapped themselves around each other.

'You smell good!'

'Of what?'

'I don't know – just very good.'

Bruno smelled of freshly baked bread – every morning. She used to inhale his warm scent and slowly feel herself go heavy in his arms and drop off back to sleep.

There is no going back.

It is Carol's birthday today. She is sixty-three. She has spent ten years with Bruno and now it is just her in the king-size bed with the view to the east over the town. Just emptiness where Bruno used to lie and gently snore and smell of bread. She buries her face in his pillow – still a faint smell of him – she has run out of tears.

It has been a month since she found him dead in his armchair. Headphones still on, an old episode of Star Trek playing on the computer.

'How could you do this, Bruno? Just die like this.'

No goodbye, just gone. They had both survived this bloody pandemic just for him to die now of a heart attack.

Elke Heckel

When she got out clothes to give to the undertakers she had found her birthday card and a gift for her in the drawer where he kept his bow-ties. After she laid out the clothes – she went back for the card and the gift and placed them on the kitchen table. They have been glaring at her since.

Today is the day! She sits down. Her flaming red, silky dressing gown is wrapped tightly around her. He loved to run his hand down her spine where white cranes were dancing across her back. He would rest his hand on her sacrum or wrap his arms around her from behind when she was making the morning tea. Kitchen love.

Now it's just her hands wrapped around a cup of Darjeeling tea. The wind seems to blow straight through the window and straight through her. The gulls still flying backwards, the pigeons in free fall until they find the next upwind that allows them to soar.

She exhales – first the gift. Heavy, a long box, wrapped in iridescent paper. His tooth marks on the Sellotape catch her by surprise, the pink champagne less so – it is her birthday favourite. It is the card that scares her the most. Her name in his neat writing in purple ink: 'Carol.' She strokes the name gently. Exhales again and then just rips the envelope. He had made a card for her from one of his photographs. A picture taken when they walked by the sea front and got drenched by the spray of the most magnificent waves. They had laughed so much.

She braces herself, exhales slowly and opens the card:

My dearest Love
I hope you enjoy your special day.
Sparkle, dance, and inhale all the beauty around you.
So grateful to have you in my life.
Yours forever
Bruno

She inhales and the smell of a mouldy lemon offends her senses.

'I hate this smell!'

Elke Heckel   68

Her aversions used to amuse Bruno. He used to call her 'Carol the nose.' Where is it? Finally she finds it at the bottom of the fruit bowl. Dried, shrivelled, grey green dust stuck to the bottom, buried under the squidgy mango, some mouldy peaches and an avocado long past its best, only the apples from New Zealand still looking ok. Fruit was Bruno's thing.

She loves avocados though. An avocado prawn salad for her birthday? With pink champagne? She has eaten only crackers and peanut butter all week – the casseroles left by thoughtful friends and neighbours have long run out. All of a sudden she feels ravenous.

She sighs and takes the bowl to the sink. Everything apart from the red-cheeked apples goes in the bin. She washes and dries the turquoise bowl bought on their first holiday in the Peloponnese. It is chipped on one side and she places it so that the chip won't show.

She tears a piece off the pink envelope and starts writing a shopping list in her scrawly writing, 'Fruit, milk, prawns, avoc...' The pencil lead snaps, as her hand stabs the paper and she howls – she won't be buying fruit and milk – no need now that Bruno is gone. She steadies herself by leaning onto the table looking out at the gulls – how she would love to join them – gliding on the thermals and screeching, screeching – carried off with her despair.

Instead she grabs a shopping bag and wraps herself into her bright red mohair coat – off to battle the elements and the shopping aisles of Waitrose in search of the perfect avocado. ⁄⁄

Elke Heckel

The Coal Women

We had just boarded the Coalfield Express in Dhanbad without a seat reservation. I was relieved that we had found seats for the first leg of our journey and was looking out for a chai-wallah to celebrate our success with tea. My friend put a dampener on my delight by explaining that we would be fined and turfed out if the conductor caught us without the right ticket. I was just digesting that piece of information, when a commotion erupted further down the carriage.

Huge sacks were being hurled into the train and moved down the corridor at great speed. Amidst the usual pre-departure hubbub it was difficult to see who or what moved them. As the commotion moved up the carriage towards us I could see the cause; sacks filled with coal were being shunted down the carriage propelled by the feet of small, wiry women in pink sarees, who sat on the floor and pushed them along with alarming speed and formidable power. They rammed them under the seats with little regard for shoes, feet or other items in thei way. I looked at my Hindi-speaking friend in surprise and in hope of an explanation. She was chuckling to herself before translating the exchange between the coal women and the passengers for me.

The pompous man whose wife wouldn't budge for us earlier was protesting: 'What are you doing here? Get away, this is my seat!'

A quick retort was hurled his way together with the coal: 'Surely you are sitting on your seat, not under it, Sir?'

This was followed by: 'Your seat? Are you going to take your seat with you when you leave this train?'

I laughed out loud and nearly didn't move my legs fast enough to avoid the next sack that landed under our bench. Others were being piled into the Western toilet.

What was going on? My friend explained these business-savvy women act like the coal-wallahs that we sometimes see on our morning walk. Unlike the men who are propelling three enormous sacks of coal on their push bikes up to fifty miles from the coal mines to their domestic customers, the coal women carry huge sacks of coal on their heads. The women have their own distribution system and use the aptly named Coalfield Express and Black Diamond to take the coal further afield for domestic sales. Both are part of an illegal but accepted network operating in the coal-mining belt of Jharkhand in North Eastern India. They get the coal from families of 'coal thieves' who bribe the guards of the open cast mines. These families eke out a very precarious and desperate existence living off the coal and suffering severe health problems and social deprivation as a result.

Our ninety-minute car journey to Dhanbad had taken us through Jharia, not just infamous for its open cast coal mines but also for the underground coal fires that have been burning there for over a hundred years. Jharia is one of the biggest towns in Jharkhand. Its inhabitants are living on top of a man-made volcano. It is even hotter there than in other parts of Jharkhand; the earth belches toxic fumes and threatens to swallow whole neighbourhoods. Plans to rehouse people run woefully behind schedule whilst the number of those needing to be rehoused has doubled in the last twenty years. Everything is covered with a fine layer of soot and even in the pink morning light the usual vibrant Indian colours appear sullied. A once white abandoned Ambassador has morphed into a London Black Cab and no one has bothered to paint over the ubiquitous advertisements for bright white 'inner-wear' and new white light switches here. As we are passing my friend tells me that a fortnight ago a woman and her twelve-year-old daughter had gone out together for their morning toilet when the daughter had turned round to find her mother gone, literally swallowed by the ground. I try to imagine this as we close the windows and turn on the air-conditioning.

Finally the train pulls out of Dhanbad. We pass through a landscape dotted with spring-flowering palash trees, their fiery orange-red, claw-like blossoms pointing up into the sky. This is the state flower of the still young state of Jharkhand, dedicated to the two-headed fire god Agni who has powers of destruction and renewal.

Elke Heckel

Heather Curwen

Heather Curwen is an artist and writer living in the Hertfordshire countryside. Her work is inspired by the patterns and rhythms of the landscape which surrounds her home. It evokes her belief that nature retains the imprint of past lives which connect with us through found fragments and pockets of energy.

Acknowledgements:
The title of 'I Drink Like an Astronomer' is from 'A Table of My Own'
by Vahni Capildeo.

Just a Girl

She sits in the prow of the boat like some kind of figurehead. This thin girl who shivers in an old blanket that smells of goats. Her face seasick green. Her hair and robe drenched with sea spray. Many are the sacrifices we made to help him bring her home – the comfort of our homes, our lovers' arms – and huge is the price we have yet to pay. Already the gods show their anger with wanton Aphrodite for starting this madness. Our muscles – knotted, agonised, slick with sweat – strain to keep the boat and this 'treasure' on course through waves that fizz with their wrath. We are angry too – although we say nothing – resentful not just for what we left behind but also for the doom that hangs over this mission. A great war is coming – a war when the gods themselves will take sides – and we are afraid. We fear not only for our lives but for the loss of the world we know. Meanwhile, Paris sits in the stern, pale, grim-faced. He screams orders at us over the noise of the wind and waves. This boy. This spoilt brat who always gets what he wants. What does he think now of Aphrodite's prize as she retches into the boiling water? Does he think she's worth all this?

I, History, say she was a seductress. Some, I know, deemed her a sorceress, thinking she bewitched Priam's favourite son. He, they said, would never have done such a terrible thing otherwise – cause so much death. For others it was the betrayal of her worthy, glorious husband – and hence her race – for which she must be damned. But I, History, love a story of duplicity. Has it not always been the woman's fault – in circumstances such as these – ever since the world began? Why look further? My scribes, who recorded this day, wrote pretty words about her face. Her eyes inspired many a couplet – rhyming and otherwise. Whole sonnets extolled the beauty of her rosy lips, her velvet cheek, her lustrous hair. I had to make her special if I was going to blame her for the war that followed. All that brutality and the loss of so many heroes – Patroclus, Hector and 'godlike' Achilles.

Heather Curwen

Because of this, men said she was irresistible. And their women called her a whore.

How it really happened will not be recorded in the Book of Time. Long before we reach Troy, they will have already decided I'm to blame for the carnage that is following us. Nobody is brave enough to blame a goddess for starting a war, so it will have to be me. The fact that Paris and I are really pawns in a game of Olympian chess won't cross their minds. No. Not for an instant. What's more, no one will consider what it was really like to be me. How I was sold for a chest of gold, in return for lands and favour, to the great Menelaus – already an old man – when I was barely more than a girl. They will not consider what it was like to share his bed, to live under the harsh regime of the Spartan court, to dwell in the shadow of the House of Atreus with its deadly curse. They are so entrenched in rigid customs and their fear of the gods that they will not see this thing whole. It will take many centuries for someone – a woman, surely a woman – to understand how it felt, while living like that, to receive the attention of a handsome stranger, and to see me for who I really am ... just a girl who fell in love with a boy and saw a chance to escape.

Heather Curwen

My Vagrant Heart

My heart sorts through trash cans,
and picks up fag butts.

It sleeps in subways,
on park benches,
covered in newspaper
and old blankets.

It roams the woods at midnight,
lies down on bare earth,
waking in the morning
stiff with frost.

Why do this? I ask,
when it could be warm, at home, in bed. ⧚

The Forgetfulness of Snow

I feel the not-there-ness of you today,
watching the leaden sky
release its burden of snow:
snowflakes dissolving
on my tongue, like ice cream.
A footprint.
An illusion.
A shape shifting.

Snow changes things.
Seals us in a blanket of forgetfulness,
soothes us with its silence.
Even crows don't call when it's snowing.
Hunched in treetops, temporarily pied,
perceiving greater wisdom in its pulchritude.

To fall asleep in a snowdrift,
and wait out winter
like some small animal.
Not to feel this emptiness,
this uncertainty,
this notion of far-off pain.

This Christmas –
when hoar frost garlands grace the trees –
I'll lay those memories in a casket of ice
and let them be stolen
by the Spring melt. ⁄⁄

Heather Curwen

The Raven Queen – a Fairy Tale

I saw her standing in front of the mirror today and I wanted to slap her. Hard. I wanted to pull her hair and pour something sticky over it. Black. It has to be black – and permanent. Something it will take the rest of her life to get out. I want her to wake up one day and look in that mirror and see all that youthful loveliness gone. Smug little bitch with her smooth complexion and rosebud lips. I vowed then to wipe that sweet little smile off her face, and I will. Oh yes. I certainly will. And soon. Very soon.

Later, in my boudoir – lying on my fox pelt counterpane – I closed my eyes tight and searched my mind for nasty things. But nothing came. More evil was obviously needed, and I didn't care how long it would take or what I needed to sacrifice to make it. I am the fairest of them all. Everyone knows it. And nobody is going to take that away from me. She's just a temporary interloper and she has to go.

I wrapped my cloak about me, the one I stitched by hand from raven's feathers, reciting an incantation at every stab of the needle. And – hat upon head – I made my way to the top of the hill where the wind blows wild and free, and voices are silenced. 'Come, my servants, and bring me bad things,' I cried, my voice ripped from my throat by shards of freezing air. For a while nothing happened; the air was clear and bright. Then I saw a shadow gathering on the horizon and their voices, at first a hum of composite sound, then individual voices announcing their presence. And so, they came. My emissaries, wheeling and tumbling in the air. 'We come, oh Mistress, at your command,' they muttered, louder and ever louder until their cries seemed to fill the sky. Their leader alighted before me and bowed as is the custom. 'For the Fair One,' he croaked and placed before me a perfect apple, the peel as red as blood and shining like a virgin's smile. But as we all know things are rarely what they seem. ✎

I Drink Like an Astronomer

I drink like an astronomer from the goblet of night,
intoxicated by that velvet blackness.
Stars spangle.
Sherbet in my mouth,
exploding in a sparkle of fireflies.

I taste the full moon too –
its liquid silver pours through my throat
like crisp wine,
like peppermint,
cold on the tongue
and all the way down,
to lie warm in the soul. ⁄⁄

Heather Curwen

Mourning for Icarus

I see you

     tumble away

from me

     burning...

        in free-fall...

Our hands   stretch out

     to touch

    but miss.

It's not written in the Book of Time
for us to be together –
now.

Next time we tread this earth
I'll save myself for you,
swathed in silk and lace,
waiting for the chance encounter
that will explode in a shower of sparks.

Then we'll stay entwined,
one limb with another,
all our days.

I think this, watching –
as the sun sinks west
waiting...
until
the last
ray
from
that
fireball
disappears
from
sight.

Heather Curwen

Judi Sissons

Judi Sissons has published poems and stories in anthologies. She taught Creative Writing at the University of Hertfordshire and founded The Writing Space in 2012 to support personal and professional development through coaching, creative writing and wellbeing. She is a member of NAWE and Lapidus. She lives in Brighton and writes poems on the beach.

www.thewritingspace.co.uk

Acknowledgements:
'Hermits' was first published in *The Spaces Between Us*, edited by Kathleen Morgan, Jamie Stewart & Oz Hardwick. (Indigo Dreams Publishing 2021).

An area of social deprivation

Forty years on, I'm running a workshop
on the allotment, a community garden
between the graffitied garage block
and the railway. Trains rattle past,
cherry green tomatoes
tremble on the vine.
We're digging deep for words,
turning over years of hard clay,
unearthing memories,
when I discover you, my lost diamond,
glinting in the sun,
behind the hydrangeas.

You brought me here
to the wrong side of the tracks,
your home, an end of terrace
propped up by the council,
crammed with siblings, food and care.
Your mum a dinner lady,
dad a postman. You wrote love letters
I could never receive.
My prep school polish
hid an inner deprivation.
My town was a lace handkerchief
politely arranged to conceal despair.

Now I sit in a moment of stillness
beneath the white noise of power lines,
feeling the sun's heat cherish my skin.
I remember how your light electrified
and dazzled me. An ancient breeze
drifts in to break the static.
In the distance the bass notes of engines,
the drum of the road harmonises
with the squash flower's yellow trumpet,
its bulbous fruit bursts into song
and dances with the celebratory bud
of a single rose. //

Judi Sissons

Exile

These nights I sleep on floorboards, far away.
Your forgotten gaze slips through in tongues
of electricity. My whirring body
remembers heartbreak, a pressed suit, crisp,
white shirt, open neck revealing the pulse.
Lately I wake automatically
into a deep think –

                  don't bother opening
curtains. I'd like to stay this way, touching
the time body of a poet, forget
myself in some self-imposed war dance.
Once I had to turn away, embarrassed
by the angular face and old-fashioned
accent behind the bedroom blind.
It could take ages to be young again. ⁄⁄

Judi Sissons

Hermits

I watch you grapple, can't tell if you're coming
out or going in, your house on your back.
We connect through a slice of blue light.
I'm still submerged at low tide and the phone
is not waterproof. You clamber onto the roof,
arms and legs flailing as each wave washes
over us. We don't understand the rules
of engagement. I worry about quicksand,
notice pockets of liquefaction,
test the ground with a toe. You rearrange
the furniture I am afraid to touch.
I can't read your body language, focus
on your mouth, eyes down tell me you're not sure
there's room for us in your minimalist lifestyle. //

Monacella's soul

Outside the cave I watch her crouch to pray,
submit to the illusion of safety.
She is no ornamental anchoret,
her impulse to hermitage driven by distraction,
a slow affinity with solitude.
Unafraid, I hide in her skirts not for protection
but to show her how the hare rejoices,
invigorates limbs, propels hearts to vibrant flight.
When soul seekers come to her for prophecy,
she leans against the washbowl, intrigues them
with visions, as she rinses dishes, dries flatware.
At night I creep undercover, nestle
in her gown, my pelt against her skin,
delve into her wildness, her only law vitality. ⁄⁄

Judi Sissons

Negative Traits of the Wasp Spirit Animal

The sole survivor of a warrior race, I slide my hairless body between red velvet, contort my petiole to slumber in your folds. My enterprise – to visualize the scooped shelter of the tribe in which to replicate the lost dynasty, reconstruct a palace of profound proportions, to seek the intimate place, assemble my own size, a microclimate in the vastness. All winter I summon the sacred geometry of hexagons, the shallow corners where my dutiful daughters will perform their labours of genetic love. Between the square and the circle, I am architect and geometrician, in love with transitional shapes. I conjure complex forms beyond experience, intuitively work in three dimensions, trace the earth measure of my lines to intersect the circumference, unveil hidden symmetry at the centre of the vortex.

Some days the light plays tricks, through closed eyelids, stirs me to fantasies of flight, to wake and claim my sovereignty, translate my unconscious geometry and rebuild our world from the shredded remnants of hope. I long to slice the sickly, saccharine squares of Battenberg, divide them into equilateral triangles, leave the marzipan till last, savour the sweetness. I never forget a face, can recognise the jawline of my rival queen, beneath her crack-head hat – her pulpy lips and lemon peel skin loom luminescent through my dream.

I have problems with authority. Arouse me and I'll perform for you, a disorientated astronaut floating in undefined space. Get too close and I'll become a terrorist in your home, chew fibres from your favourite manuscript, spit out the tears of motherless children. I will paralyse your limbs and drag you to my chamber – feed my sugar addiction. //

Quarantine

Exiled along the landing for daring to be ill,
as the choir practises psalms in the hall below.
Panic sings in my head, synchronizes
the rattle in my chest, reverberates windows.

No holding hands or mother's gentle words,
familiarity is forbidden in the sick bay.
Cold linoleum, stripped, white walls, metal bed,
the scent of infection laced with Dettol.

Now, fake leaders on their quilts of contagion
airbrush me from the empty streets,
where those who have no bed lay in doorways,
the future closed until further notice.
Downstairs, someone is coughing
and fear runs faster than a wild hare's bolt. ⫽

Judi Sissons

Vixen

I pause the movie, let the tap run cold,
wait for the kettle, half full, half empty.
In the dark street below my window, a car slows,
turns the corner. For a moment I feel
normal. Make tea. Then remember. Rewind.

Fast forward. I lean out into wide night.
No one sleeps as screens flicker in the glow
of homes across the city. Above the silence
the shadow world scratches close outside.
I swallow a damp lungful. Fade to black.

Credits roll. Invading shapes loom
in the communal garden, men jostle a girl
pleading for her fix, upstairs someone phones the cops.
A scream cracks the air, ricochets
off apartment walls, the thrill of her raucous bark. //

Judith Biddlestone

Judith's qualification as a state-registered nurse initiated a career working in hospitals and clinical teaching. Following marriage, motherhood, and setting up home in several countries, she's surprised that her hobby-writing of poetry and prose constantly reflects those years working with the patients and staff that populate her earlier memories.

Lifeline

Private Kenneth Logan, son, friend and brother, kneeling in the chaos of ambush in Gleeson's hotel, County Derry, digs his fingers in to stem the gushing crimson flood from the bullet wound that has ruined his best friend Barry's heart. Tangled on the blood-soaked carpet in this wreckage of a half-century of 'Troubles', Kenneth lowers his cheek to Barry's mouth, praying pointlessly for a warm ripple of breath in the now silent flesh.

Kenneth Logan, home in South Shields, doing his best to erase the memory by drinking away his entire army discharge pay at Wetherspoons, punches out his anger on yet another staggering Saturday night. But this is the night Kenneth gets bottled back. As the phone rings on the little table in the chilly narrow hallway with the news that will batter his Mam to bits, Kenneth's trachea is breached by the casualty doctor and intubated to compensate for the severance of the spinal cord by a well-aimed bottle of Newcastle Brown Ale.

Quadraplegic Kenneth's only weapon is spit. Silver gobs dribbling, stickily glistening and pooling around his bed. New nurses try to comfort and tidy but soon back off. Kenneth hates being touched, although in reality he has no choice about that.

At bath time, strapped into a hoist and winched above the bed, his flaccid body swings, the rasping whistle from his tracheostomy his only scream. Nurses instinctively mouth-breathe to manage the secretions, excretions and furious silent tears. In his four-wheeled prison Kenneth grimaces and spits and hopes his erection will catch their eye.

At visiting time the family comes. His sister Shelley sits in the doorway picking the bleeding skin around her thumbnails and craving the end-of-visiting bell. Mam strokes Kenneth's soft, paralysed arms, offering up exhausted forced smiles, clumsily shielded grimaces and nauseating vodka fumes. Little nephew Stevie balls his well-behaved fists and longs to finger the tracheostomy hole.

Yellow rubber gastrostomy feeding tube surgically inserted into Kenneth's stomach and stitched neatly into his abdominal wall becomes an umbilical cord, his lifeline in this dystopia. Kenneth can't swallow, which puts paid to fine dining. A round dietician reads out the prescribed feeding plan above the constant blare of MTV. Creamy green or yellow liquid becomes his daily sustenance. Under Kenneth's tortured gaze, sunny nurses crush and swirl the endless crumbled drugs in watery hospital milk and syringe them down the tube. The dietician watches attentively, holding the alphabet communication board, as Kenneth spells, *You're a useless piece of shit, just like all the fucking slop.*

Spit and impenetrable resistance defeat speech therapists, frustrate occupational therapists, enrage physiotherapists, and cause the chaplain to doubt his faith. As the year turns around daffodils reach up, erect and strong along the bordered driveways outside the high sealed window. Inside, the staff avoid the flying gobs and attempt a discussion on the possibility of bringing a little relief to the frustrations of Kenneth's paralysed existence. They plan a weekend at home.

They mobilise the right support: nursing care, robot bed, hoist and straps, feeding kit, suction tubes, barrier creams, rubber sheets, plastic bags, laxatives, diarrhoea relief, alphabet communication board and lip balm. Kenneth spells out, *Leave me alone, you selfish cunts.* Positive he'll benefit from the change of scenery, they wave him off on the Friday in his motorized chair, spitting in the lift and choking at the rush of cold fresh air.

A borrowed electric bed fills the tiny front room. A bank of plugs and wires spaghetti the floor. In the small hours Mam sits and stares, red-eyed, as her Kenneth wheezes through his gaping neck, dozing on his tranquilizing medication, waking briefly at the rattle of ice cubes in her vodka glass.

Saturday morning brings the early district nursing shift. They count and crush and push his drugs into the tube, evacuate his rectum, suction his lungs and park his chair at

Judith Biddlestone

the window where he spits at the trees in the square, scrubby garden that was his playground as a boy.

Mam pops next door to fill them in on how he is. Shelley sits at the chipped Formica kitchen table in her stained dressing gown pushing the heels of her hands into her eyes, paralyzed with fear for their future. Forcing herself to look in, she sees her Stevie climb up Kenneth's still body to hug his face and she knows she's got time for a smoke out the back.

Stevie loves uncle Kenneth's alphabet board, helpfully pointing his chubby little finger where Kenneth's eyes swing then focus. He's good at this, so when Kenneth's eyes dart across the board, Stevie's enthusiasm for a challenge drives his swift cognition. He instinctively embodies Uncle Kenneth's rushed but precise instructions. As Shelley shuts the back door and resumes her vigil at the table, Stevie triumphantly replaces the bottles and syringe on the scratched sideboard next to the photo of Uncle Kenneth in his army uniform. When his uncle starts to doze, Speedy Stevie gambols out to climb the trees.

Coming back through, Mam watches for a moment as Stevie climbs and waves like her Kenneth did as a bairn. As she heads in to relay best wishes from next door, something catches her ear; a new silence hangs in that room's fetid air. Grey bubbling froth oozes from Kenneth's natural and man-made holes and onto his fresh T shirt. For a single magical moment Mam takes the convulsive twitching of his head and shoulders to be a miraculous intervention, a renewal in answer to her bleary prayers.

Again the blue lights spin and shriek. Next door haul little Stevie safely in to save him from the pointless, frenetic battle in the tiny sitting room. Neighbours stand on spotless doorsteps shaking their heads, nicotine-yellowed fingers dabbing with hankies in relief that their sons are safe inside on ketchup-stained sofas. Breaking free from Shelley's shuddering grip, Mam grabs at the body bag on the high trolley, falling and bloodying her swollen knees on the broken flags as stomach-sickened paramedics squeeze out through the latch-less gate and away. //

Judith Biddlestone   98

Maureen Tully

Maureen Tully
always in a hurry
to the nurses' home
where you hide all alone.

As you dust each day
the other nurses say,

Maureen Tully,
were you ever in a hurry
to remove your tights
in romantic lights
with a nice young man
who if encouraged would have ran
his eager cheeky tongue
where it caused most fun?

As your thermal vest slips
and reveals the bits
that he'd want to tweak
to make you shriek
licking flesh that's weak
causing fluids that leak,
could he bring you to a swoon
in your spotless room?

With your tights in a ball
you could wave him down the hall,
breathless for the day
when he comes back to play. //

Judith Biddlestone

My Waitrose

You cannot know how much you satisfy
my urgent need for fresh and frozen food.
I'm drawn to you no matter how I try
to stretch the household budget as I should.
I can't control the pull to deli cheese,
nor yet ignore plump chickens on your spit.
If chocolate choux can bring me to my knees,
and tempt my tongue to sample, so be it.
The flush I feel at squeezing perfect pears
will far outweigh the guilt of paying more.
And when my card can't take the strain, who cares?
Be sure within the week I'll come for more.
This quiet life can be a little dull,
my newfound joy? To see my cool drawer full.

Principles of Above-the- Elbow Amputation

The flesh is opened up below the point where bone is cut,
skin, fat and muscle conserved,
healthy blood supply preserved.
Foreshortened neurones are tucked away from harm,
(ensure embedding is tied off tightly,
or phantom pains cause screaming nightly).
The suture line will be just fine over time if it's wrapped
above the point where the false arm's strapped,
(mimic the folded foot flap on a baby's sleeping sack).
Insert drains, pad with gauze and bandage round,
pressure dressings tightly bound.
Cleanliness and comfort count,
but a handsome stump is paramount.

Tom was flailing, furious, as doctors, toiling, curious,
fought this lump in his right humerus.
Doppler vessel readings show a marked increase in blood flow
as cells of his sarcoma grow.
Future treatment plan reviewed, all bony cancer drugs now used,
histological findings prove the amputation pathway true.

Tom's hands:
an interface for world and brain,
equal age and loved the same.

Left hand: wedding band, a hand to hold with less control,
useful when swimming, cavorting and cooking, nominated best
supporting role.

Right hand: precision grip, sophisticated finger tip, cortex-led,
cognition-fed,
rising to salute the great, essential to communicate, a must for
pleasure,
digging treasure, intricate work and games at leisure.

They prep Tom's arm with expert care, flesh shaved bare,
painted brown up and down,
with iodine, chlorhexidine.
Dry it off with sterile towels, skin sore, feeling raw,
glistening,
like plump organic chicken skin.

Judith Biddlestone

Wrapped in red material
stamped *antibacterial*.

On his way to surgery
half asleep, half awake, dreamy medicated state,
he lifts the arm, and turns the palm
towards his lips, a sleepy, gentle goodbye kiss. ⁄⁄

Down Below 1976

Gynae wards are tiny tribes of women,
getting fingered by the doctors till they're sore,
oestrogenic hormones tested hourly,
fallopian tubes sufflated until raw.

Examinations cover labia majora,
Bartholin's glands, fibroids like giant beets.
Women healthy from the waistline upwards,
while pathologies are staining all the sheets.

Endless tea and biscuits while the chat goes on till dawn.
Deep friendships form among the most forlorn.
Men shuffle in as visitors, embarrassed and withdrawn.

Ovarian cysts
ballooning zeppelins,
crippling, disrupting,
fluid collecting,
hormone rejecting,
women accepting
the discomfort of crippling pelvic pain.

The surgeon excises
cervical disease.
Worrying and waiting,
nurses placating,
colposcopy grating,
numerical rating
more puzzling than the haemorrhagic flow.

Then there's grieving for a uterus removal,
as malignant cells spread out, a spider's web.
Pelvic clearance is the only way to treat it,
plus kleenex as the endless tears are shed. ⁄⁄

Judith Biddlestone

Kate Cook

Kate Cook writes short stories and poetry and has recently completed her first novel. She is based in London.

Optimists

An untimely lack of caution proclaims *Happy 90th birthday!*
in buoyant silver and pink, right outside Marks and Spencer's,
moving those who dodge us, as we sail by, clutching
familiar expectations. We hurry on, impatient to meet

the inescapable smile she wore sixty years ago, or more,
when she was still the one they hoped to bump into in the street,
or at the coffee-house where fatal freedom hitched a ride.
We too will defy our airborne destiny,

like she did in the weary wasted winter of '57, when she almost
stepped under a bus, only a busy woman pulled her back
with just a *Watch where you're going love!*
becoming her best friend, for all of thirty seconds.

A woman who was not her mother but deserved to be, on that
day
when salvation wore a green raincoat and pushed
a tartan shopping trolley. Birthday bustled today by
we who know nothing of her fault lines, she rises

from her undoing chair to celebrate the chances she had to do
better than she might have done, all things considered.
The effrontery of our ballooning congratulations
reminds her of how far she had to fall,
but didn't. ⁂

Ostreia*

You are, and were, the finale. Layers of briny satisfaction
lie heaped at our feet but, moved along, we succumb
to clipboards and questions, none of them the right ones.

We can pick you up, but only at the end, as they did.
We wonder whether anyone has touched you since you were
emptied out, then dumped with your brothers and sisters.

Your clatter is the only complete echo of what was here.
The rest is cracked and scattered, pixelated dolphins severed
from their tails, dismembered gods drowned in mud, piece by
piece.

Scrapers cannot scrape them back into the glow that civilisation
requires,
but you are unchanged. You could have arrived this morning,
transported in the white fishmonger's van, for our elevenses.

My fingers curl around you, just like those of Marcus Aurelius
who was clean and content, just as we are. Perhaps we are not
quite so clean, grubby progress in the shires.

Almost breaking bread with the long dead, village kids in flares
jostle the better class of hyphenated townsfolk who clung on
to an empire that was beginning to falter.

Romano-British outlines leave us cold like the Frigidarium
but sharing a morsel moment of excavation moves
these nine-year-olds to wonder. We too will become shells

of what we are today, living at the edge of a life much grander
than is customary in this corner of our home county,
then cast off, into the dark. ⁄⁄

*Edible oysters

Kate Cook

The Policy

Roland was not living up to his job title. A chorus of critical voices accused him of failing them, of failing everyone, even those not yet born. He was made to feel as if just by doing his job, an important job of public service, he was personally responsible for planetary doom. It was deeply unfair, especially as others who might have been given his post, like George or Linda, would have been so much worse. Particularly George.

The new name was the problem, well part of the problem. Why did he have to be called the Minister for Future Success? It was an invitation to failure. Something more attainable, 'Minister for Reasonable Efforts in the Face of Catastrophe', would have been safer.

'Follow the science,' they all kept saying. Well, that was all very fine for schoolgirls and hippies, but who was going to pay for the science, not to mention the roads, the pensions, any of it? It was not called black gold for nothing.

'How do you even get to a protest if there aren't any bloody roads?' He said this out loud to himself. Made audible however, it was not a persuasive argument.

'Roland, this is a delicate balancing act, I hope you realise that,' the PM had said when appointing him to his new role. 'We are not *for* fossil fuels, we are not *against* fossil fuels.'

Roland had waited, as he knew he should.

'We are *for*...transition. This is truly a moment of transition.'

'Yes, I see,' said Roland.

As Roland had read up on the Paris Agreement on Climate Change, thankfully not a very long document, he added hopefully, 'a *just* transition?'

'Hmm, tricky word "just",' said the PM. 'Trades unions will see it one way, the boards of oil majors another. Try asking the birds and the bees, what would they consider "just"?!'

Just in time Roland registered this last comment as a joke and laughed heartily. He tried to join in: 'or the polar bears or the rain forest!'

The PM raised his eyebrows. 'We keep away from both of those,' he said firmly. The meeting had ended there.

Things had started out, well, mixed. Roland's arrival at the Department was greeted with mild interest in the press. He was neither the best, nor the worst, person who could have been appointed to lead the new Department so there was not much to grab the media's attention. Roland felt that there was more to him than people realised and decided to make a ripple, a reasonable and proportionate one. When he had attempted to square the oily circle with a new and really quite enlightened policy on fossil fuel subsidies, legal proceedings had immediately been issued. Some people were never satisfied, it seemed.

He thought, just this once, he might get some sympathy at home. He made his opening gambit at breakfast the day after court papers had been served.

'The newspapers have picked it up, not a very balanced account.'

He watched his wife as she looked at her phone, reading up on the case. She was engrossed.

He poured a cup of tea and passed it to her.

'They are like, like ...greyhounds.'

He was trying to express the thought exactly but, as usual, she cut across him and spoiled it.

'So that makes you the hare.'

'No, not me, that's not it at all. The *policy,*'

'Oh, I see. The policy.'

'Yes, we all agreed it. The PM thought it would do the job nicely. A way of launching the new Department and it is my role...'

'Yes, do remind me Roland, I always forget, are you the Department for Future Success or the Department for a Successful Future.'

He was beginning to sulk so she softened a little.

'All right, please explain it to me. What is the policy?'

Did she really care or was she just after him again? Perhaps he was the hare.

'Everyone wants us to stop subsidising fossil fuels, coal, well that has pretty much gone...oil and gas.'

'Why do you subsidise oil and gas?'

Roland groaned. Could she not, just this once, join the debate at the right point?

'All right, just tell me what the policy is.'

She had spoiled it now. It would sound as though the policy was just a fudge when actually...he felt very tired.

'Well, we are going to phase out *inefficient* subsidies. Actually that's been agreed for ages...'

'Then why not do it?'

'Because we could not agree on what inefficient means.'

'But you had already signed up to do it.'

He ignored that. She was wilfully not understanding him.

'We are tied to gas as a transition fuel, you know, the transition to net zero emissions.'

'And they don't like that?'

'Actually no, it's far too slow and we will almost certainly overshoot the... but wait until I explain, that is not the policy.'

'I thought you said it was.'

'I mean that is not the specific policy that they are challenging.'

Silence, at last.

'Well, they're always on at us to comply with human rights so we have devised, no we have *established* a detailed model that shows how each unit of subsidised gas contributes directly to the fulfilment of human rights, specific ones, um, let me see, girls' education for example.'

'Couldn't you have solar-powered girls' education?'

She was a hypocrite. She did not really care about it. It was just the latest stick to beat him with.

'I am going into the garden.'

She was still reading the article.

'They seem to be rather successful, your law firm. They also represented that chap who was being denied compensation for...'

He was out the door. He noted the 'your'. She was getting meaner and meaner.

He walked down to the clump of oaks at the end of the garden and drew a long deep breath.

'Oh God.'

He turned it all over again. Some progress was better than none. He was the one that had pushed back on coal and that had not been easy. There were plenty of investors who still wanted…it might not make him a public hero but that was because the public did not realise how very hard some of this was, what he was up against. At least he actually cared about it, contrary to what the letter before action had implied: …*Notwithstanding his professed commitment to human rights when on the Select Committee…now apparently indifferent to the plight of millions of displaced people…floods…wildfires…he had once declared that the sanctity of life was paramount but now….*

Very personal and not at all appropriate, he thought. He looked up at the slightly too green leaves. They were lime green really but they were never represented that way in pictures. He did care about these things, he really did.

'I have no one who understands,' he said, breathing more deeply. Why was he doing that? Was it a panic attack? But no, he felt remarkably well and much more expansive, more rooted than he had done for ages. Firmer too. Perhaps the Pilates was helping after all.

'I understand you, Roland,' someone said.

What a marvellous voice. With a voice like that you could really go far in politics. Such an unfair advantage, a voice someone wanted to listen to and you were half way there. His was rather nasal.

'Do you really?' he asked.

The sun was in his eyes, blasting through the branches directly above. A lot of light when it was normally so shady. His throat felt very odd, on his tongue was a sweet taste but also something earthy, aromatic. A bit like that ghastly non-alcoholic gin his brother-in-law always insisted on bringing over.

He smiled. Just knowing that someone understood, appreciated and had noticed. It was the sort of feeling he imagined people had when standing before Her Majesty, as he himself hoped to do one day. That would keep her quiet. Not her Majesty of course, perish the thought. He shuddered

Kate Cook

at the very idea. No, the girl he had married. Not a girl anymore, no longer a twig, more of a bough. She was so heavy now, a weight on his left side and always shedding. What was he talking about? He realised he was gazing at the sun directly. Perhaps that was why. It felt so good, so very good.

'I love you,' he said to the sun. 'I know I don't always say it but I really, really, love you.'

'I know,' said the Sun kindly, 'but please try to focus, this is busy time of year for you. There's a lot going on…'

'Yes, there is!'

Empathy washed right through him, pouring into his stomata.

'It's the litigation that tips the balance, you see. It is so stressful, all the advice I have to take and the lawyers always refusing to say what…'

'Shhhh,' said the Sun. 'No one litigates against you. You have only one set of tasks. They are unchanging and that is what you should be thinking about now.'

'Yes, you are right. It's going to be a good year.'

He relaxed, perhaps he dozed off, then suddenly awoke to a sharp repetitive sound, or was it a touch. He could not make it out but it was slightly obscene and intrusive.

'Stop that right now!' he said.

'It's just the woodpecker,' said the Sun.

'I don't like it. It feels horrible.'

'But it does not do you any harm. On the contrary, keeps the wood-boring insects under control. Relax and enjoy the sound of your enemies being consumed.'

'Well, in any case, I need to leave now, I have a meeting to get to.'

'That has been taken care of, Roland,' said the Sun. 'Now just photosynthesize'

It sounded like the most wonderful thing anyone had ever said to him. It felt like the most wonderful thing he had ever done.

'I could do this all day,' he sighed.

'And so you shall,' said the Sun.

The Minister for what his colleagues snidely referred to as 'Some Sort of Future' was late to the cabinet meeting, but to their surprise he did not look embarrassed. He just took his seat and smiled at them all. Then he stretched out his hands and gazed appreciatively at his fleshy fingers, flexing them in turn. He rubbed his whole hand over his face with obvious enjoyment.

'Oh for heaven's sake, Roland,' said the Education Secretary under her breath.

She had once been an ally. They had entered the House at the same time, were the same age and positioned themselves similarly on many issues but, at some point, Roland had lost his edge. She had not. This morning though, he looked energetic. He almost rippled with well-being.

Another one to watch out for, she thought; it was becoming exhausting. Just when you thought someone had stalled and started their inevitable descent, they bubbled up again, welcomed back into the camaraderie of predestined success. Her success hung on what she had said in the last five minutes, at every meeting.

Roland leaned back in his seat and watched a tiny spider stroll across his blotter. His item was about half way down the agenda as usual. Just at the point when everyone began to switch off and await the arrival of tea. It was always his fate to compete with the biscuits. This morning however he had something to work with. The prospect that his Department was about to be taken to court might arouse slightly more interest than his matters usually did. It was, in some perverse way, a matter of pride that a leading law firm had focussed its attention on him. At least, that is what he would have told himself once but, today, none of that seemed to matter. He was quite content to wait and let things develop at their own pace.

For the first time since his appointment to the Cabinet, the potential for connection was there, it was palpable, though more evident under the table than above it. He tentatively reached out and touched the foot of the Minister for Transport who was sitting next to him. Without speaking

Kate Cook

he was able to convey the urgent need to cooperate, not just with each other, but with the fungi which surrounded them.

The Minister for Transport was momentarily startled. He knew Roland had been under a great deal of strain. He really has reached his limit, people whispered. Next time around, said others, calculating where they would be left when this Minister was felled and a clearing opened up. Sunlight in which to grow. The odd thing was, the Minister for Transport felt he understood exactly what his benighted colleague meant. They all needed to extend themselves. This was a message he too could pass on, but perhaps more easily if he kicked off his shoes.

Slowly, under the table, as the cabinet worked steadily through the day's agenda, socked feet met stilettoes and stockinged feet met handmade loafers. Italian leather rubbed against something a little more in keeping with not quite post austerity Britain, and in turn reached out to a bunion or, in one case, an uncomfortable case of plantar fasciitis. It was the same each time, the jolt from an unexpected encounter was allayed by the warm conviction that this was the right thing to do. While arms and hands gesticulated gently above the cabinet table surface, under the table much more was afoot. Connections made, alliances for future, intertwining for resilience, against pests, against drought, against erosion of all kinds. From the bottom up, the Cabinet finally took collective responsibility for the forest they now realised they were.

The PM beamed at them all over a bourbon. It was too sweet, he thought. He wanted something earthier, a charcoal biscuit perhaps.

'And now for the Minister for Future Excess!'

No one laughed and the PM felt the joke fall away from him, shrivelled and dead.

'Please, Roland, do go ahead. Are we ready for another courtroom joust?'

All heads turned towards Roland. That felt right, up to a point. They would solve this together, genuinely joined up government.

'Thank you, Prime Minister. Well, we need to take a broader view of the entire issue. There simply aren't enough of us to keep the air flowing as it should. So much depends on us, we provide shelter, food and simply a place to be, to millions.'

They were almost with him, a little confused but not baffled. The work going on under the table, the intertwining of rhizomes and the understandings thus transmitted were having an effect. Some of those connections were becoming permanent. The Minister for Transport slipped his toes into the soft leather of one of the Trade Secretary's handmade loafers. Fits me like a glove, he thought. Only the Education Secretary seemed to be holding out. Roland smiled at her and suddenly she seemed to understand she could not manage this alone.

They all gazed down at the French polished surface of the table. They did not want to end up like that.

'Rewilding?' offered the PM tentatively.

'Half-earthing, Prime Minister.'

Roland felt this was a reasonable compromise, given what they were up against. The faces around him looked hesitant.

'Room for biodiversity and for humans, all of them. We will finally have to learn to look after each other,' said Roland. 'No more "how the other half lives", no more "bottom billion". No more overconsumption and profiting from other people's poverty.'

He sat back. The Minister for any Future At All Would be Nice had said enough. They all understood, at last.

'Only half?' asked the Chancellor.

'Mustn't be greedy. An arboreal rebalancing of the books, that's all. ' said Roland, the Minister for an Increasingly Assured Future.

'Where will we all live?' asked the Minister for Housing.

'In proper homes,' said Roland. 'The Department will engage new special advisors who actually know what they are talking about. Forest dwellers will pass on their wisdom to new forest dwellers…and no more investing in cutting down our brothers and sisters from other canopies, anywhere in the world, is that clear?'

Kate Cook

Everyone nodded. The Minister for International Trade hung his head in shame and fiddled with his pencil.

There was enough energy for all of them, Roland explained, if no one hogged it all, and this would renew their hopes.

It was good, they could see that.

'Um, what about me?' said George, the Minister for More of the Same, or Even Worse.

They all looked at him sadly.

'We have had our fill of you,' said Roland.

'Indeed we have,' said the Secretary of State for the Oceans and Fisheries

'You have done more than enough already,' added the Minister for Health, sternly.

'Although may I just say...' said the Foreign Secretary, but they all turned and stared at him so he coughed into his sleeve.

George felt keenly that his own unique contribution was about to be passed over. He had to speak up.

'The research we have been funding, on solar radiation management, is really looking very promising and there are also the aerosols, which I am told will keep global temperatures at a very comfortable...'

'Smoke and mirrors, George! Such bloody nonsense!' boomed the Prime Minister.

The others all joined in the laughter. The very idea, deflecting the one thing they all depended on. Separating them from the source of all that was good and perhaps causing rot, decay, desiccation and irreversible shadows.

'George, we already have an army of geo-engineers, as many as we need, provided they have room to grow,' said Roland.

'And are not cut down in their prime, undoing all their life's work into the bargain!' added the Foreign Secretary, who finally seemed to have caught up with things.

George felt the ground slipping away. He needed to make a concession, a manageable one.

'Well, we could certainly plant some more trees, quite a few of them, why not?'

The Minister for Science adjusted her spectacles and turned towards him.

'Plant a few more and then watch them burn up, as of course they will, the way things are going, won't they George?'

George said nothing, it seemed best. He was never quite sure when she had finished.

'Forests old and new will burn, George, and they will keep burning until you stop stoking the furnace. So you must... just...stop.'

All movement under the table had ceased and everyone looked despondent. George could not think of anything to say.

The PM decided to bring this to a close. It was sunny outside and he really needed to be out there where he belonged; it was imperative, in fact.

'That's settled then. No more hocus pocus in the skies and the only drilling down we will be doing is with our meristems!'

They laughed, though not loudly, mainly they swayed and, under the table, toes tentatively curled around each other, springing back to life.

The half-earthing announcement was made by the Prime Minister that evening in a special address to the nation. Then the storm broke.

Opinions were sharply divided.

'Visionary,' said some. 'Verging on insanity,' said others, while the headline 'Cracked!' was followed by a plethora of speculation on the state of the PM's health.

The Cabinet Secretary put the whole thing down to the air conditioning and ordered an internal inquiry into building maintenance. The PM, always rattled by unfavourable reviews, put it down to his new vegan diet and put himself back on red meat. The press buzzed around it all for the whole of the next week.

But somehow the idea had embedded itself and kept reappearing in odd places. Schools started to put forest skills on the curriculum and one of the oil majors redesigned their

Kate Cook

logo as a tree morphing into oil. The 'original tree of life' was to be the new slogan until an indignant NGO for the preservation of ancient orchards issued proceedings, claiming trademark infringement of their own logo, and spoiled everything.

The odd thing was, no one was sure what to do about the PM's proposal. It seemed to leave stubborn little shoots in the most inconvenient places.

The PM was having his daily garden walk with his chief advisor. He had become obsessed with woodlice and kept picking them up and tickling them until they became little armoured balls of rage.

'An inquiry, a judge-led inquiry,' said his advisor.

'How will that help?'

'Pick the right person and they will find a way through and take their time doing it.'

'Through the thicket then?' said the PM wistfully.

'Trust me, Prime Minister. I have someone in mind.'

She was indeed the perfect choice. Respected, apolitical, good on women, naturally, and a mathematician.

'Ticks every box,' said the advisor to the PM, as he finished the call. She had agreed, warmly but without undue enthusiasm just the right tone.

'They have asked me to lead the half-earthing Inquiry,' she told her husband that afternoon.

'Will you have to be away much?' he said, without looking up from his screen.

'Not sure - possibly.'

She walked into the garden. This always made her feel better. She stood among the silver birches and sighed as she watched a flock of long-tailed tits jumping from branch to branch like excited tourists ascending an ancient tower. The birch forest extended up into the blue like an old Russian folk tale, taking her somewhere else entirely.

She had always disagreed with A. E. Houseman on this point, cherry trees could not hold a candle to these, her favourite trees.

Kate Cook

'*You* are the loveliest of trees,' she whispered to the birches, looking up into the shimmering canopy which had begun to waft around her like a crowd of old friends, and then it dawned on her. 'Yes, I am.' She felt herself bending in the breeze with her new companions and happy to do so.

Far down below, she noticed a small figure walking briskly across the lawn and back into the house, clearly with much work ahead of her. ⁄⁄

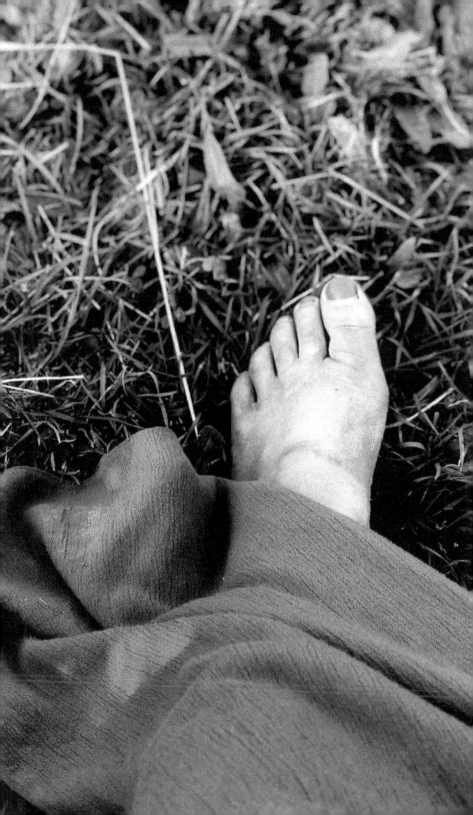

Rebecca Bailey

Rebecca's ambition is to go feral and never wear shoes
In the meantime, she insists on foraging food, bones
and stones, growing plants, collecting useful jars
and poking things most people wouldn't go near. Her
writing explores relationships, death (in its many guises)
and transmutation.

Red Flag No.1

Are you pissing in my kitchen sink?

Body stiffens. Caught.
Cock in hand. Still pissing.
No!

I can see you.

Micro pause. Processing.
Confident shake. Zips.
Boys pee in sinks, it's normal.

Laughing.
One in power.
One in surrender. ⁄⁄

The Carapace

I find myself on all fours. Flint stones, sharpened by force, cut into knees as bodyweight buries my bones in sea-sodden pebbles. From my wave-hewn dais, the breakers boom and bellow below. Baying. Braying. Searing white noise. Hair whirls and spirals across a shame-flooded face, dragged to the surface and laid bare for the gawkers. Guttural grunts heave from slack-jawed mouth, summoning whatever's left of my putrefied soul to disgorge itself onto that freezing shore. To flop and squelch and squirm amongst the broken scallop shells. To be whipped clean by salt-heavy spray thrown like holy water from a priest's vial. A smooth pebble creeps beneath my palm. I cling to it. Curl my fingers around it. Press it into myself with knuckle-white force. The other hand finds something similar. I grasp my faithful rocks as if hanging onto the core of the earth itself, pulling raw energy from liquid stone. I ease back onto haunches, raise my head and let out the banshee. And I slam those stones together. A crack of agony and defiance. A crack of punching rage. A crack to sound the rancour of twelve years stolen, of poison and torture meticulously drip-fed and main-lined in equal measure. A crack to signal a soul syphoned, vampired into non-existence. A crack for the carapace crushed and cochinealed. A fat drop of water falls from the sky, slaps the back of my hand. A memorial tear to soothe the seared palm forced and held on heated foil and the roasted flesh of another consumable creature. One of many unrequested lessons, scorched deep. Never again. The rain comes to wash anything left behind. I sit. I breathe. I am. //

Rebecca Bailey

Undertow

I watch the lapping foam graze my boots. It's not that I want to die, per se. More that I find it increasingly difficult not to dissolve myself. Reorder atoms. Experience existence as a tempered tuile wave shushing a lonely pebble tossed to shore, whilst oil tankers call mournfully from the milky distance. Or understand how it is to sink and sit in the silent depths to dream of all the things that I will become, until I'm disturbed by the lantern of a passing anglerfish who'll waft my molecules to the surface once more. To be the rageful froth that hisses and spits and claws at the barnacle-sharpened hull of a tiny trawler, tossed between a rock and a cold seabed as the tempest wages war from above. Or to feel the soft, silky tug of the insistent current that will usher me along the corals, where I'll coax and soothe soft creatures who hunker from harm. I watch the lapping foam and decide again that it's no better or worse than where I am now. Not different enough to warrant the undignified hauling of a bloated shell made ready for stick-poking, anyway. *So be it*, laughs the seagull. *See you again next week. Yhaah?* ⁄⁄

The Darkest of Places

'What made you finally leave?' That's what I'm asked the most.

I want to tell them something big and exciting to serve their justifiable curiosity. Feast them with the story of how our neighbour, tired of listening to violent rages spilling into the hallway, called the police on him – how he was led away in handcuffs, whilst I was wrapped gently in a warm blanket and given hot tea. Or regale them with how there was a dramatic rebellion where I stood fiercely in defiance, eyeball to spit, delivering some measured and legendary line, leaving him as small and pointless as I had come to be.

The truth is, it was neither of these things. No way as close or as straightforward. But I wish it had been. It would have given the cold hard evidence needed for others (and myself) to believe the grave reality. Or my soul something to cling to in the bastard months ahead – some form of fight-back, some form of retrieved dignity, a tiny fizz of power regained to keep me from slipping back under the surface of this cesspit existence.

So no, it wasn't one brilliant jolt into freedom. No dashing grand finale. It was hundreds upon hundreds of micro movements, played out in a body and mind that were no longer my own, painfully slow transgressions to regain some semblance of self, each with their own particular punishment for daring to dream of a different way of existing. 'Wilfully disobedient,' that's what he used to call me, on a good day anyway.

A decade in captivity. Seven years writing myself notes to counteract 'that didn't happen.' Two years' secret voice-recording to hear the tactics in flow. One septic appendix. One beloved pet dying in my arms. One completely failed escape attempt. One partially successful escape bid. Countless conversations with 'friends', silently begging to be seen:

'But if you two can't make it, none of us can.'
'I know he's hard work, but you're really good for him.'
'You sure it's not just the seven-year itch?'

Rebecca Bailey

'Has he ever hit you, though?'

Pandemic. A different kind. Bringing new kinds of death to endure. Lockdown One's abuse served with a daily dose of alcohol. Lockdown Two's served with the added spice of cocaine. And then came the threat of Lockdown Three, where I knew I wasn't going to make it out alive this time, by his hands or my own.

It took a couple of years' research into domestic abuse for me to accept it. A year building strength of character. Six months learning to 'grey rock'. The regulation emergency suitcase packed and stashed. The warm hand on my back, showing me the way out. A single shaky text taking up the offer of a spare room. One rescue date set. And the most beautiful line I have ever read:

'Stay strong, sister, we're coming for you.'

What made me finally leave? Audacity, I guess. The infinitesimally small voice, squashed deep inside my core, whispering, *This was not who you were meant to be*. The lucid vision of a split road ahead: one straight as an arrow, set in an endless dust bowl desert, with a small oasis every hundred miles, repeated, for eternity; one almost imperceptible to the untrained eye and set in an unknown quantity – an untrodden jungle path, vibrantly verdant, filled with untold dangers, brimming with life.

Sometimes we find out in the darkest of places. It's how we painstakingly crawl ourselves out, inch by searing inch, that makes for the most daring adventures. Adventures made for a wilder heart. ✎

Sunday Ghosts

I found a tatter of me today
blowing blissfully down the road by Enterprise Car Rental.

The sun nestled into her bed-worn hair, bare feet padding warm
concrete,
as she returned from the bakery with an oven-warm loaf,
to feed you with, when you finally awoke.

You'd eat brunch together on the balcony,
sip French-pressed coffee made belligerently strong,
watch cars and people shift and flow on the street below,

until the hangover's eased enough to gather Bloody Marys. Then
to the beach,
where you'd read her stories from Gerald Durrell,
with each character played in full.

And she'd wish with all her heart that the book would never end,
that she could make this her happy ever after.

I found a tatter of me today,
acting so frivolous with her careless mind,
as she lost her way, unknowing.

I left her in the gutter, torn and shredded.
amongst the desiccated fragments of you. ⁄⁄

Rebecca Bailey

Sarah Newington

Sarah Newington lives in Brighton and began writing seriously during lockdown. Having written off and on for years, experimenting with different forms alongside so many wonderful people allowed her to explore and clarify ideas about a singularly challenging but ultimately very inspiring time.

Awake unto Me

It was the beginning of the summer holidays and a green Suzuki Jimny bowled down the street, trundled up onto the pavement and stopped. A girl in her mid-twenties swung out of the driver's seat, jumped down onto the pavement and slammed her hand onto the roof of the car. 'Right, you witless pricks – out.'

Twenty feet above, Madeleine Cresh, who had been sitting on the floor of her bedroom in the overlooking block of flats, looked up.

An older man stepped out of the passenger's side and looked at the girl, one hand resting on the top of the door. 'Darling, if you don't mind …'

'Dad. It's a joke. Come on, old man – bring Granny with you.' She rapped on the back window, still looking at her father. 'Hello, Granny! Get out now.'

Her father sighed and looked down. 'You know your mother does not enjoy that particular epithet.'

The girl laughed and slapped the window once and then looked inside. 'Mum.' She stopped smiling and thumped the window. 'Out.'

Madeleine had moved from the floor and was sitting on her bed, looking down on the scene below. Another equally boxy car had parked behind the first and the tops of seven heads were scattered across the pavement, noisy but completely static, like a game abandoned by a child.

'I drove so I'm not lifting anything – sorry.' The girl raised both her arms and crossed them at her wrists, stepping sideways between the people and the luggage clogging up the pavement.

Madeleine stared down at the girl as she flashed in and out of the trees in the neighbouring garden below. A person with plenty of private-school health and height and who moved and dressed like an off-duty show jumper, she was the leader of the newly arrived group and Madeleine hoped that they wouldn't be staying long.

Later, in the early afternoon, they came out into the garden in ones and twos and Madeleine went back to the window. The dad was there and she could hear him but she didn't mind. Next came two women in their early sixties, both wearing brightly coloured gilets, their fingers stopping up the tops of a clutch of Birra Moretti bottles.

"Scuse fingers!' one of them trilled, as they nestled the drinks between candlesticks and dip. The architecture of the flats that surrounded the garden trapped it in a pool of sound and Madeleine could hear every word that they were saying.

By the following Saturday, the group had sat in their garden from lunchtime until one in the morning for six days in a row. The noise was intolerable and it was the sound of the girl that Madeleine hated most of all. She had a false, yucking laugh that impaled all other conversation and she spent all day calling the others 'no marks' and swearing at her mother. Madeleine had decided that she would write a note, telling them all that the noise they were making was persistent and intrusive and that she hoped that they would consider this while they were outside. The man who lived on the floor above her had shouted down to them the night before, saying they had ten minutes to shut the fuck up before he called the police, to which they responded that it wasn't late and to calm down. While Madeleine had grinned with relief and glee at this exchange, it wasn't her way and she would write. It really couldn't go on any longer.

The day that she wrote the note, Madeleine had been lying in bed feeling unwell. She had been given an inoculation the day before and had sweated and shivered under her open window for hours, listening to them. Feeling dizzy and hot, she wrote the note out on an envelope that she'd fished out of the recycling, then wrote it out again on a piece of lined paper. She pulled her white canvas shoes onto her bare feet, picked up her keys and as if on castors, went down to the house.

Imagining that she would post the letter through their front door while they were safely in their garden and out of the way, Madeleine was horrified to see that the rest of the garden curved round and ran parallel to the street, bordered by a long wooden trellis. Not having seen this from her bedroom, Madeleine blew out her breath and felt too warm. The front door to her right was PVC plastic which surprised her and she couldn't see anywhere to post the note.

'Hello?' she called. The people in the garden stopped talking, staring at her through the diamond slits of the trellis before someone laughed and they started again. Feeling small and outnumbered, Madeleine seemed to have wandered into a secret society – the preamble to a Kubrickian sex party or something dreamt up by Lovecraft, a summoning of sea creatures in business suits. She stared back at them, sweating, when a single voice called to her.

'Rosy? Rosy, come in, you stupid cow!'

What was wrong with these people? There was a tremor in Madeleine's chest like a plucked string and she held up the paper. 'I'm not Rosy. I've got a letter to deliver – do you have a letterbox?' They kept laughing.

She was about to try again when the father came jogging through an archway in the middle of the trellis. 'I'm sorry,' he smiled. 'We're prattling on.'

She smiled back and was glad it was him but she felt cold, as if she belonged to another species. 'I've got a note to deliver.'

'Oh right?'

'It's about the noise,' she said, holding it out to him. She saw a flash of her own father then as he tapped his temple and his face creased into a pained squint, and she felt like crying.

'Right.' He shook the note out. 'Fair enough.'

There was silence between them and Madeleine stepped back. 'OK, thanks,' she said. As she walked back to her flat, she heard the girl.

'Dad? What did she want? Was it about the noise? *Really?*' The emphasis at the beginning of the last word turned it into the insufferable cliché that Madeleine detested and she saw herself turning back, screaming into the garden and throwing herself on the girl. But the dad – he'd been nice. The dad would sort it out.

But, for the next three days, the noise continued and at nine o'clock in the evening on the third day, the opening bars to a song that Madeleine barely recognised tinkled with the fairy lights that had been unceremoniously strewn amongst some branches. Sitting in the window, she closed her eyes in fury and disbelief as a thin treble voice rose up to her window sill:

Beautiful dreamer, wake unto me,
Starlight and dew drops are waiting for thee,
Sounds of the rude world heard in the day,
Lull'd by the moonlight, have all pass'd away!
Beautiful dreamer, awake unto me.
Beautiful dreamer, awake unto me.

It was an old song by Stephen Foster called 'Beautiful Dreamer' that Madeleine vaguely knew and had liked, but they had destroyed it now and the thing that had been holding her together snapped. She stepped up onto her bed but the scream that she knew would never come out caught in her throat and went back down again like acid. Why *shouldn't* I scream at them? Her thoughts cracked one after the other, like a line in splintering ice. Why can't I put my fists through my window and jump down? Why can't I press my thumbs into their eyes and smash the back of their heads open on the edge of their firepit? They're doing what they want to, so why can't I? She put the fingers of her right hand between her teeth and bit down as hard as she could, breathing through her nose. By the time she'd stopped and taken her hand away, she had decided what to do.

When she got home from work two days later, Madeleine saw four boxes stacked up on top of the wooden shoe rack by her front door. They were large and together they made a dreadful monument to what she had planned and for a moment she regretted what she'd done and was afraid, as if she'd ordered four bombs. But like most things that are delivered nowadays, the packaging was superfluous to the thing that it was meant to protect and she smiled when she looked inside.

In her bedroom, she unpacked four tiny black bluetooth speakers and wrapped each one in insulation tape, meticulously covering any lights that might give her away. She connected the speakers to her current phone, two old phones and her computer, sent a text to her boss saying she was ill and wouldn't be in the next day, sat on her bed by the window and waited for it to get dark. When the last light from the house below was switched off, Madeleine put on her shoes, picked up the speakers and her keys and opened her front door.

In her neighbours' garden, she pushed one speaker deep into a bush that ran along the fence opposite the trellis before climbing into a tree and wrapping another one in a purse of leaves and sticking it into the elbow of the highest branch that she could reach. Next, she stepped onto the back of a bench, reached up and taped the third speaker to the inside of a metal pipe the colour and texture of the bottom of an old pan and then she was on the grass again, running to the shed opposite the house where she taped the last one behind a security light.

Controlling the speakers from her bedroom, Madeleine played 'Beautiful Dreamer' from 6 pm until 3 am every day for the next two weeks. The volume was never very loud because she liked the thought of her neighbours wondering if there really was music playing or if they were going mad and she didn't want to disturb her other neighbours, who were innocent. There was furious shouting and searching for the speakers but they were never found because she often went down in the middle of the night to move them around or take some away for a day or two. The girl looked for them the most and Madeleine watched her for hours.

She had decided that everything would stop on the night of August 20th. It was 2.20 am and she felt hollow and was glad it was ending soon. She had done what she wanted now and through it all, the image of the father's face when she'd handed him the note hung like a dim shadow at the corner of her eye. He hadn't stopped the noise, hadn't helped her, but Madeleine had seen him in the garden by himself, with his fingers pressing at the middle of his forehead as the music played and she had cried watching him. So she was tired of the game now, and longed for the morning when everything would be over. It felt like when she'd been fourteen and stayed up late on Friday nights watching Eurotrash, desperate to learn about sex, this thing that seemed as distant and cosmic as the stars but feeling thinned out and disgusted. Or later, when she was at university and awake at five in the morning, surrounded by stale-breathed men whose skin sweated out cheap wine and cans of Red Stripe, willing one of them to signal that it was the end of the interminable Charles Mingus sessions that she loathed and time for bed.

She pressed the side of her phone and looked down, her eyes smarting painfully as the screen lit up in a ghastly square. She couldn't hear the music but she could see the small white dot that showed the song's progress, inching like larvae across a single white thread. She looked to her left and down and saw that the automatic light over the shed door had come on. She threw her phone face down on the bed and edged further out of the window.

'Seb, you dick. Get your phone out and put the torch on. Dad's calling the police tomorrow because it's harassment and I want to be the one to find the speakers.' The girl. Madeleine heard a boy mumble something and the girl replied.

'You are actually thick as shit. Go in and get it.' In that moment, Madeleine changed her mind about how to end everything and didn't care what happened afterwards.

She stood up and walked to the full-length mirror on the other side of her bedroom, picking up the white throw that covered her bed on the way. She imagined she was standing before an altar as she arranged herself in the semi-darkness; it covered her completely, from the crown of her head to her toes and she was pleased – a bleached Virgin Mary. Then she turned on the light and walked to the head of her bed and sat down where her window panes met in the centre; the

Sarah Newington

light from her room irradiated the garden below and her window had become a mirror. With legs crossed and hands resting on the window sill in front of her, Madeleine smiled. She had gone into the garden at almost this exact time yesterday and taken back all of the speakers and they were lined up on the sill in front of her like obedient children. She turned all four devices to maximum volume, made sure that the Frank Sinatra song was at the beginning and then turned them on, one by one. The noise was deafening and Madeleine beamed, pushing her windows open as far as they would go. Every bar was a parade of ballet dancers that should have been quivering on the springs of little girls' music boxes but had now been snatched up by a malevolent hand and the notes that had been pitched to sound like glass and pearls were a fistful of discordant, nightmarish twangs.

The girl in the garden below looked up. 'Oh my God.' She sounded different now, like a real person. 'Oh my God.'

Madeleine smiled down at her and lifted the same hand that had held the letter all those weeks before, but that now held her phone. She rotated it as far as it would go to the right and then the other way and she felt the bones in her wrist click. She disconnected three of the devices one after the other, so that only one was left playing. She put her phone down and placing both hands on the glass, touched her forehead to the window and mouthed Foster's final line, looking at the girl:

Beautiful dreamer, awake unto me.
Beautiful dreamer, awake unto me.

Twenty feet below, the girl dropped the phone she'd been holding and the two of them stared at each other, each bathed in their own light; the girl, a hare caught in the shed's security sensor that pooled around her and Madeleine high above, backlit on her phosphorescent stage of pillows and wood.

Staring down at her, Madeleine thumped the window once as the girl had done, smiled, disconnected the last speaker and turned off the light. ⁄⁄

May the Angels Lead You into Paradise

Gwen Gallo had been teaching for seven years and had never met another student like David Thomas. A twelve-year-old boy who had been in her class for two years, he had become the subject of a set of elaborate stories that she and a fellow teacher, Matthew, had devised during their daily journey home from the secondary school where they worked. Driving down tree-lined lanes that glimmered in the slanted light of a five o'clock sun, they would joke about how he wasn't a child at all but a messenger, an alien blend of angel and celestial prophet who had been sent to Earth to assuage the afflictions of all humankind and to lead it to salvation. An all-knowing cosmic empath, he had come to save them all.

Always the last to leave after every lesson, David would slot his books into his rucksack with the care of an archivist, while his classmates spilled into the corridor without him. He was relatively tall but slight, his hair was the colour of cream and the helix of fringe that whorled between his eyes was touched with gold. Quiet and deliberate, he barely spoke.

Every day, Gwen arrived at 7:30 and rarely saw any children until at least an hour later. On this particular morning, she was late and was desperate to get into her classroom to sit down and put her makeup on before having to go downstairs to the weekly briefing. Sunglasses clamped between her teeth, her lanyard, badge and keys dangling from fingers that held a grimy cafetière and thirty-four exercise books corkscrewing in her arms, she battled with the door.

'Christ almighty,' she whispered, as the key that she'd fumbled into the lock span round uselessly. It finally caught and she went in, chucking everything on the table.

Gwen looked up as an accordian of books slid onto the floor and she saw David Thomas standing at the furthest side of the room, facing forward behind the seat he usually sat in, three rows from the front.

Sarah Newington

'David!' she breathed, pressing her fingertips to her heart and laughing. 'What are you doing? How did you get in? Why did you lock the door again?'

He was completely still and didn't answer.

She knelt down and picked up the books before putting them back on the table. 'It's very early, sweetheart,' she said. 'Do you need me for something?' He didn't reply and she stepped forward, her coat half off, hanging from the crooks of her elbow like a vestment. He didn't move.

'David – are you OK?' She waited. 'David,' she repeated, frightened. 'Come downstairs with me. What's wrong?'

He lowered his eyes and his lashes shimmered in the May sunlight that coursed in through the bank of windows. 'I'm all right,' he said.

Gwen shook off her coat, relieved, and walked back to her classroom door. 'Do you need me?' she asked, her hand resting on the handle.

'No.' He looked at her then and his eyes, which were a naturally heightened blue, were positively dazzling. 'I don't need you but you need me for something. I've come to help you.'

Gwen kept the door open but took her hand away, trying to remember if she'd forgotten to do something. 'Really? That's kind. What – '

She broke off. David was still standing by the window, but now he had moved to face his teacher. A cloud of opalescent light was marbling between them; an aureate tapestry with plumes of coral and ivory, it swelled and pooled before Gwen's eyes. At the centre, the iridescent image of a person who she hadn't seen for two years began to emerge – the person that she longed to see most in the world but never would again. Her boyfriend of five years and love of countless before, he had died two summers before but his face and form had remained a constant. Occasionally a comfort, it was mostly an aching reminder of what had been lost and his memory had become blighted, turned into a dogged apparition by her turmoil and grief.

'David,' Gwen whispered, clutching at the collar of her dress, her mind fusing and flickering.

The boy looked at her. 'He knows that you're all right because he comes to see you sometimes.'

'Who? What are you saying?'

'Him. The one that you wrote the letter to in your diary after he died. You wrote that if he needed you he was to come to you in your dreams. He says he's going to stop now because he thinks it frightens you. He says he doesn't want you to be scared or sad and to carry on.'

Gwen dropped to the floor, a supplicant to the boy's words and the light between them.

'He says don't change anything and carry on. He says that he's free and very happy and that you must believe him. You said to him that if you only ever loved him then that would be enough but he says he'll watch over you to make sure that doesn't happen. He says he'll keep you from those that would do you harm but that you must promise to carry on. He says it's better to have had what lived between you than not at all and to keep going.'

Gwen reached out a faltering hand and her voice was cracked and small. 'I don't understand.'

'The three of us know that you do understand,' the child replied. 'Don't be afraid. You were right about me. I've come to help you.' He reached out as she had done and a lustrous finger touched hers. 'In paradisum deducant te angeli.'

Gwen covered her face with her hands at these words, gripping at her fringe. The Latin line that David had spoken came from the Requiem Mass that Gwen had sung many, many times, in stuffy, overheated practice rooms and cavernous French abbeys. She had practised her part over and over again, learning it by heart and imagining that these ancient words would be her beloved's induction into where she knew his illness would ultimately lead him. She took comfort in them and pretended that she would be the one who would deliver them as she stood under the vaulted solemnity of stained glass and staring saints during endless rehearsals. The day after he died, Gwen wrote it out on a piece of ivory card and stuck in on her wardrobe door, with

Sarah Newington

> Your cause of sorrow
> Must not be measured by his worth, for then
> It hath no end

from Shakespeare's *Macbeth* written underneath, one of the few lines from English literature that meant anything to her. After this, she would write it out mindlessly, again and again, in meetings or during ponderous phone calls with friends, and she had offered it up instinctively when she and Matthew had been deciding on what David would say when he and his cosmic plan were ready to be revealed.

Gwen's hands were clasped in her lap, resting in the folds of her dress and she gazed up at the ineffable glow. 'Please. Please help me,' she whispered. 'I don't know what's real.'

'Don't be afraid,' David said again. He touched the coalescence of light between them with his finger.

'Are you telling me the truth?' Gwen asked, her cheeks enameled with light and tears. 'Please,' she beseeched the boy. 'Please tell me that this is real.'

The child smiled. 'Of course it's real.'

Gwen lifted her chin and closed her eyes, glimmering in a sun of peace and relief. Then she nodded, her palms pressing at her chest. 'Who are you?' she asked.

The figure before her smiled and took his hand away, his face beatific with kindness.

'I'm David.' ⁄⁄

Susannah Underwood

Susannah Underwood is a parish priest in the Church of England, where story and metaphor is the native language. She has a particular interest in Dante and the journey of our inner life. Susannah is married and a mother and writes from her study in Dibley.

Acknowledgements:
'In Praise of Rescue Hens' after 'Jubilate Agno' by Christopher Smart.

In Praise of Rescue Hens

For a daughter's heart-break deserves a ridiculous gift.
For a trip to a poultry scrapyard shows her many are spurned.
For putting birds in a box as if they were books makes us laugh.
For as we drive home she carefully cradles a hen's hope of
happiness.
For she names them like aunts – Petal, Patsy and Pam.
For they have wings not fingers so she needs to open their coop.
For she has to get out of bed.
For she is rewarded with eggs.
For eggs mean pancakes and pancakes mean syrup
and syrup is sweet on her lips like kisses.
For their comforting counsel of clucks.
For they say buck, buck, buck when she greets them.
For they are in love with her.
For she has corn as a gift and they know her gifts are golden.
For their bottoms are bloomered.
For their crops are caramel and chocolate and cream.
For their throats purr and brood and rumble joy.
For they say never mind dear and all is well.

For they rescued her. ⁄⁄

Ash Wednesday

The passion flower in the Australian bush
needs fire to cleanse and bring about new birth.
So too this oil and ash upon your brow
takes you to death, you creature of the earth,
reminding you of your sure mortal end
so in death's embers you will not remain,
but Son-kissed by the greeting of a friend,
you will arise – a phoenix from the flame.

Remember you are dust and to dust you shall return.
These words are life although they sound like death.
The potter takes the clay and shapes its form,
and you are recreated by God's breath.
So shrive and die again into this soil,
and grace will germinate through ash and oil. ⫽

Susannah Underwood

Knitted

I knit you, small child;
your form, a soft knotted skein,
lies cast from my cord,

draped and drawn to fit
your shape; you are no bind,
your skin warms me.

I am patterned by
pacing in the moon-spool nights
and your needled cries.

You permeate me –
milk-sleep, blossom, soured malt.
I smell of your skin.

Your laughter colours
me – threads gold, ochre, honey
from your tickled ribs.

In you I am stitched.
Loose gently. My greatest fear is
we will be undone. ⁂

Playing

It was my mother's decision that I learned to play the violin. For her it was a childhood dream never accomplished. Her mother, widowed at a young age, was determined her two daughters would be equipped for self-sufficiency in their adult life and decided piano would be a more useful instrument for a teaching career. So that was that. Incidentally, she was right.

I'd always envied the girls with small flute cases who sat neatly on the school bus whilst I clambered past, my shoulders weighed down with the cruelty of a Thursday timetable that insisted on PE, Home Economics *and* music in one day. My body was patterned with the criss-cross of bags: the faux-leather straps of my Tammy Girl satchel; the sports sack, heavy with hockey kit, whose thin strings cut into my neck; the long purple cheesecloth shopping bag draped over one shoulder knobbly with tupperware boxes, each containing a vital ingredient for a macaroni-cheese-meal-for-two. Amongst these my violin bounced while I tried to make my way up the aisle to the back seat, the cumbersome case colliding with every girl who sat on an aisle seat of this school coach.

'Sorry. Sorry. Sorry,' I resignedly murmured to my disgruntled looking peers. Although deep down I knew it should be my mother issuing the apology.

Lying on my stomach across my pastel pink and grey geometric patterned duvet I carelessly flick through Smash Hits Magazine, stopping on occasion to check out the lyrics of the latest Thompson Twins top ten hit, or study with curiosity the androgynous beauty of this new boy George. *This is the life*, I think. Coming across a photograph of the girl-woman band Bananarama I look with envy at their lion-like hair – backcombed, high-lighted and huge. I glance in the mirror at my own flat strands, climb off the bed and sit purposefully at my dressing table. Pulling my comb from the muddle of mini troll dolls, scented pens and scrunchies, I get to work. I take handfuls of hair and tease the ends, stopping

Susannah Underwood

on occasion to fill the air with theatrical wafts of Elvive hairspray. With each backstroke my hair grows ever larger and my eyes ever more approving as the girl who looks back at me morphs into woman.

The tape recorder next to my bed makes a sudden and loud clunk as it comes to an end. Startled, I turn to look at the door and sit completely still, listening to make sure no-one is coming up the stairs. Confident I have not been found out, I move towards the machine and press rewind. The ribbons speed back to the beginning and again my finger pushes the central button down to play. Once more the sounds of badly played violin scales travel under my bedroom door, snake down the stairs and waft into the kitchen where my mother is clearing up after dinner. I imagine her looking at the clock. *Good girl,* she'll be thinking, *only ten more minutes of practice and then she's earned her time with Top of the Pops.*

When I grew up and had my own daughter I bought her a flute. ⟍

Reckoning

Will it be a final capsizing:
souls dragged down by a life's wreckage,
swell-swallowed into Leviathan's jaws?

Will it be a spiraled Dantean descent:
eyes sealed by lament's frosted tears,
shame locked in, under Cocytus' cruel crust?

Might it be a more modern Sheol:
waterboarded, lungs fear-filled, confessions
coughed until there is enough to convict?

Or could the judgement of God be as this:
dawn's tide on pebble hearts, softly lapping,
love-kissed into colours so we glisten in the sun.

A gentle turning of the shell to reveal
a hidden pearl, our broken fragments as shingle
gathered by His waters and made into music. //

Susannah Underwood

Suzanne Watts

Suzanne lives in Hertfordshire with her husband and two daughters. She finds group creative writing exhilarating. Her writing helped her empathise with others and explores the challenges of 2020 that she felt most keenly – isolation, the climate and ecological emergency and the Black Lives Matter movement.

Acknowledgements:
'Monuments in 2020 Vision' after 'Our Monuments'
by Tadeusz Różewicz.

The Fabric of the Oil Man

The international corporate executive wears a suit of finest
Acrylan
printed with machine oil.
A snaking pipeline connects his deep pockets.
His new-on shirt is dazzling in stratospheric rayon,
around his neck a tie of Bri-Nylon,
a material that is deathless until it fragments into the tiny
particles
that feed the belly of the fish.
The blue ocean sheen of his trousers is where the fish will feed,
the warp and weft of the acrylic thread
holding them as they swallow, gulp and flail
at his feet.
His shoes are factory fresh,
the uppers smell of other material,
the sole of other material. ⁄⁄

Tingling Montalbano

Clarrie Stoakes was trying not to panic about time running out. She still thought of herself as an independent career girl and her job was as safe as it could be, working from home, But she was forty-three and single – and now it was lockdown. She did a lot of yoga to help her feel safe.

She uploaded her profile photo on the new flirting app, Tumble. The filter smoothed out some tired lines, and her makeup – copied from a Charlotte Tilbury makeover tutorial – was working well. It was accompanied by the single line:

Livia seeks her Salvatore.

It was the first week of Lockdown Two, 2020. The November afternoons had never been so dark and the cold was seeping through when Carrie saw the message pop up on her notifications.

TUMBLE: You have a new tingle.

AJ:Can I save you from being alone, Livia?

She clicked to see the sender. 'Save you' – he understood the reference to Salvatore - the 'saviour'. But did he know who she, 'Livia', was? Was he her sun-soaked Inspector Salvo Montalbano?

Suddenly her phone seemed to access a new range of functions – pre-programmed heart shapes and champagne corks flying across the screen in an unnecessary display of celebration. *Bit of an overreaction*, she thought. But up until then she had not responded to any of the chat-up lines. All of them lame, or overwrought with an embarrassing effort to sound spontaneous, confident or whatever gross attempt a guy could make to give a girl a 'tingle'. None of them could distract from her yoga poses and she had come perilously close to dropping it after her fourteen-day free trial, so perhaps Tumble was showing how relieved it was.

Suzanne Watts

TUMBLE: You have responded to AJ's tingle, would you like to check him out?

OK – here goes, thought Clarrie as she clicked Yes and a photo of AJ popped up. He was bald like Salvo but not handsome. A slightly crooked English face, a long jaw, gappy teeth that did not cry out to be smiled. His oddly-shaped specs gave him a distinguished air though – Clarrie knew they were expensive.

TUMBLE: Would you like to reply to AJ with a question? Yes/No?

CS: Yes.

Clarrie had one prepared for the eventuality of meeting a potential Salvo. AJ was in the running, despite not looking anything like the incorruptible Sicilian detective inspector. But she reminded herself that Montalbano himself was no oil painting. The inspector's mystique lay in his gaze, the casual but attentive way he listened – tiny movements of his eyes and head signalling empathy as he grilled his subjects until he graciously took his leave, or asked his right-hand man to escort them politely out of the office.

CS: Livia. Dream girlfriend or total mare?

AJ: I liked her more in the first episodes, when she was played by that actress who couldn't speak Italian and they dubbed her over really badly. She was a mare but she was real. The new Livia is an ageing Italians' idea of a Swedish feminist.

Clarrie could never put her finger on why Livia annoyed her. She was so endlessly giving, insightful and conveniently distant, providing her Salvo with occasional flying visits from the mainland, so he could get through the lonely nights and resist the flagrant attempts of sexy young Sicilian widows to get him into bed. AJ had nailed it.

AJ: Here's mine: Which of Montalbarno's sidekicks do you prefer, and why: Mimi or Fazio?

CS: Mimi the handsome lothario? You must be kidding! Fazio. He has such an air of constancy. He is completely the opposite of what you expect an Italian man to be. I love his dependability and the solemn way he looks at the Inspector. He is devoted to him, and he wants to serve him. He desperately wants to be right and correct. Some might say he is boring, but I find him more mysterious and attractive with every episode.

Clarrie found herself a little surprised at how easy it had been to express these thoughts. Where had they flowed from?

AJ: Nothing much to do with him being a slim, dark, handsome Italian stud then?

CS: Ha Ha! Not really! So, what's your idea of fun? Apart from watching Montalbarno?

AJ: Fun! What's that? I haven't had fun for months. I am 53, out of shape and when lockdown's over I'll be heading off to watch the Gunners. That's the categorical truth.

She winced. It was not what she had expected, but she had to admire his honesty. It was a challenge really, and she liked that.

AJ: Now that's out of the way - tell me your truth? What do you miss most in lockdown life?

He'd been honest so she had to reciprocate.

CS: A reason not to eat half a bar of Galaxy a day.

What was the 'guilty' emoticon? The red-faced one with the hangdog eyes? Yes – that summed it up.

AJ: Do you think you could go without chocolate for one day? What would be a satisfactory substitute?

Then Clarrie felt it. The tingle. It ran down her body and lodged itself somewhere around her sacral Chakra – the place of self-gratification. Now she just needed the will and the strength to trust AJ through the ether. She had never seen him, heard him, smelt him or felt him. But he was the first man to penetrate her inner being. ⁄⁄

Monuments in 2020 Vision

Our monuments are proud.
Their messages are not ambiguous.
But they are seen and not heard.
Time to ditch the emptiness of our monuments.

Immutable and silent,
time has moulded our monuments to be invisible
when viewed from below.
Let us put them in a glass case.

No more frozen facsimiles
trapped in their trite poses and the clothing of the past
or, their bodies publicly stripped to catch our eye,
giving permission to gaze with carnal interest.

Monuments have had their day.
History is a shifting sand.
Dare we dictate?
Let us celebrate movement instead. ⁄⁄

Suzanne Watts

The Triumphal Spring of the Woodland Town

The street in Hemel Hempstead where I live is full of small terraced houses built in a uniform post-war style. It's not pretty. There's a jumble of white UPVC window frames and everyone chooses a different style. Some are bowed to affect a cottage feel, others flat and rectangular. There is no sense of harmony or proportion. No one thought aesthetics were important in the rush to build new towns for the poor of London. On these dark brick houses is the strange cladding of rough brown tiles arranged in frilled patterns, the only concession to decoration. Alongside is a line of council-owned garages. These were built in an age where the family motor car was a prized possession to be housed away from the home. It is a little port for it to be kept clean and polished. There is a tap for the attachment of the hose at the end of each block. Now, most of these garages are empty, or used as lockups by tradesmen avoiding business rates, or full of our unwanted furniture and junk. Our cars now inhabit the paved, blocked or gravelled spaces in front of our houses which were designed to be our lovingly-tended front gardens. Two steps is the most we wish to take to access our cars. As a result of our lack of interest in movement, the space allowed in the council garage for us to open a door and get out is not enough for the average thirty-three-inch British body circumference.

Behind the garages is the third zone. It is the part the post-war planners, dreaming of a peaceful and hopeful future, got right: a small but established woodland. At night there are the calls of foxes and owls. By day we hear pheasants, woodpeckers, red kites, crows, wood pigeons and starlings. We spot violets, daffodils, crocuses, and primroses planted secretly by anonymous residents among the native bluebells.

During lockdown bored residents, unable to go to the gym, football or Costa Del Sol, looked for half an hour recreation in the woods. I would greet them on my daily walk, and become familiar with every path in the copse. Then one day, I noticed a small door painted at the foot of a tree. This was visited the day after by a plastic fairy. Then, someone decided to leave rocks painted in bright colours on a sawn trunk nearby. Gradually the offerings grew — from garden gnomes and perfect replicas of woodland animals to silver bells, cockle shells and pretty plastic maids in a row. One day, I passed an unfamiliar couple standing looking down at the collection. I passed a comment and he responded. He was amazed, he said. He had lived in South Africa, and all these things would certainly have been stolen there. I was dumbfounded. To me the objects are detritus, an unwanted surplus of bloated lives lived in a surfeit of plastic. But to an African, they might be covetable. It made me think about all the things we have. Our privileges and luxuries. The saplings planted in post-war 1950 would have looked hopeful. Spindly shoots fighting to establish themselves at the edge of a new settlement. In two generations they reached sixty feet tall and now offer life and beauty, shade and inspiration for the imagination.

In the second lockdown in 2021, people in Hemel Hempstead launched a new campaign for towns to have trees planted wherever new development is planned. This campaign is called Woodland Towns. ⁄⁄

Suzanne Watts

Yvana Reeves

Drawn to writing for the way it uncovers her ideas and for re-imagining memories, Yvana enjoys the insights writing provides. She's learnt that crafting her writing is fun, especially during lockdown, when the stimulus and creative energy of the Words from a Distance group provided a vital connection to others and to herself.

Lime Green Spring 2020

Lime green was the ironic colour of Covid. The sunniest spring in years, the loveliest of blossom and birdsong, with time to notice all the nuances. It should have heralded in a welcome time of renewal. Instead we noticed the beauty and at the same time knew what was unseen but dominated our lives and thoughts, Covid 19.

It took me time to stop calling it corvid, the family name for dark birds like rooks and ravens. That seemed apt, as the virus reminded me of Hitchcockian black birds heralding something unstoppable and deadly.

Crows and jackdaws are the benign corvids of my morning birding-for-exercise walks through lime green trees coming into leaf and bright green fairways, kept short by the groundsmen, still driving sit-on mowers over Essendon Golf Course, closed to players but open to locked-down walkers.

Alongside the smart greens, hidden by trees and scrubby vegetation are the rough paths and wild places where the golfers never walk. These have always constituted my home 'patch', the piece of countryside or urban space that each birder calls their own. Where we meander out often, usually close to our real home, to listen and linger, to skulk and wait. It's here we watch the seasons change as birds arrive from their summer or winter homes and leave when the time is right for them. Where we swirl round to follow a tiny movement as a bird zips by, hoping it will land where we can see it. If so, binoculars are focused on a mass of leaves until a sign, maybe a twig moving oddly as a bird bounces onto its perch or where a leaf takes on a certain shape as the bird tries to melt into the background. Typical clues to the presence of life. With luck the bird emerges into the centre of the eyepiece, the focus adjusted fast to capture what might only be a split second in which to identify and reverentially name that bird.

When I first tried bird watching it was movement that guided me where to look. I didn't know alarm calls and song, dismissing aural clues, thinking them too jumbled and difficult to distinguish. But over time and some good teaching I came to understand more and more about the pitch and detail of birdsong. By now, twelve years into the extra dimension to my life provided by birding, I largely listen first to find out what birds are around, then try and pick out where the sound is coming from.

'Start with the easy ones, the calls you know already, even if you don't know you do,' advised Stuart.

Who hasn't heard a blackbird sing or a woodpigeon gently coo? Stuart, shock of dark hair and with a pensive smile, was my constant bird guide and teacher, during the years of our relationship. He was endlessly patient as he shared tips and stories of how to remember some of the most common calls as we birded the nature reserves around the UK and made trips to some of the iconic birding places in Europe.

'Hear that mournful little song' – a phrase he always accompanied by a gesture of turning a handle, like cranking an early car. It denoted the kind of circular sound of a robin, endlessly grieving. Now I cannot walk the footpaths around here without hearing several robins plaintively calling and mostly obligingly hopping out to see what I'm up to.

A male chaffinch has an irritatingly repetitive song if you're around one for long. Stuart told of a time he was camping with birding friends.

'We'd pitched our tent near a river and under trees. All very lovely until we heard this call, over and over again. Now I can't forget the upcurled whistle, at full pelt, with a kind of "huitt" rush at the end. Boringly persistent but another one to know easily.'

Early on in our time together we birded in Poland, full of chemical-free farmland, vast nature reserves, hidden lakes and ancient forest. We tracked new species as we walked through the different environments: meadows abundant with wildflowers, marshes attracting swarms of insects, swiftly followed by terns eating their fill and the magical, oldest forest in Europe at Bialowieza. We saw birds whose pictures I'd only gazed at wistfully, in the Collins Britain and Europe field guide.

I remember a little gem Stuart helped me identify.

Yvana Reeves

'Hear that call? The one that sounds like "pleeesed to meet chew".'

We were crossing an old wooden bridge over a slowly meandering stream in a dense piece of woodland. Perched above the water, as sunlight was glinting through the trees, he sang his welcome. With a bright crimson crown, cheeks and breast continuing to pink wing bars, this bird is a joy to see. A common rosefinch, except it isn't in the UK. I'd never seen one but it was on my 'wanted' list. I came to see many equally lovely new birds, but I'll never forget the charm of that song.

Five weeks into restrictions the lime green changed as leaves unfurled to a more mature variety of greens, yellows and even claret. The sunshine gave way to cool rain. The skies lowered and glowered a dirty grey. Without the sun the colour leeched out of the birds and they became harder to see and to identify. But the walks sustained me as more skill was needed, which kept anxiety about Covid at bay. And there were always surprises; a distant cuckoo call, then sighting a pair, a dabchick or little grebe that decided one of the golf course's reed edged lakes was a good new home, a whitethroat perched in full view on a wire singing its heart out for a mate, a hare in a field, muntjacs on a footpath. More to notice and to enjoy, reminders of a world I care deeply about.

Sunshine on fresh lime green will be good to welcome back each spring but may trigger mixed memories for the rest of my life. //

Redundant, Still Lovely

Proud purpose lost in a century of change,
the hammered cylinder of my core now rusts
beneath its matt black shell, backdrop to my ego.
Then, fresh Far Eastern design showcased my assets
as I preened myself in gold, green, reds and mother of pearl.

Filled with light brown spills I knew my place, could see
my happy twin filled too, both ready to do our duty,
now dulled, empty, with the lingering smell of coal dust
a scented clue to our stalwart past. Curios in this present,
we watch the street or whoever comes to the country door.

In the room an open fire is laid ready, but doesn't need us
to bring it dancing to life. Instead, sulphur tips, dusty kindling
and fuel-soaked squares vie to take our job, to be The Ones.
We take a stand side by side, stiffen at the easy options and
smile
when the logs fail to catch, red tongues to rise. We know better.

I laugh, hollow as I sound, knowing my reason for being;
what I longed for, yet feared most, was the hot heart of the fire.
Trapped in retirement, I could be tipped
by a casual knock into the heat,
my proud skin melting, my very core exposed, leaving me
twisted, ugly, spent,
my treasured, faithful twin
alone. //

　　　　　Yvana Reeves

Sonnet to Silent Slough

Crocosmia dips darkly scarlet combs,
touching pale grey marble, beneath which lies
the past. Mother first, fifty years alone,
then father. They wait to hear our stories.

But their three children have no progeny,
citing careers, the Pill, things left too late.
No-one will come, keep the headstone tidy.
Ice, storms, sun will help all disintegrate.

Fifty more years and dates might reveal facts
but not the tales of tears, love, laughter,
their traditions, dreams. No flattened tracks
will carry signs of flowers placed or cleared.

For those who pause to look, who wish they knew,
the words will read: family, faithful, true. ⁄⁄

Those Crittal Windows

Crittall windows. They were the thing in 1950s housing and the black, steel-framed, single-glazed glass looked stylish. It was in the summer of 1960 that Dad and Mum moved us three children into their proud first semi.

Grasmere Avenue, Slough, next to Kendal Drive, the names echoing the same aspiration in homes that a Lakeland holiday might offer in the days before the family travelled anywhere but to a caravan in Selsey or a B&B in Worthing.

There's something anyone who has lived with 1950s Crittall windows would know. Summer is fine but by the time winter arrives you'd got to know their Achilles' heel. They let every cold blast of rain, fog or snow seep through and battle with what little heating existed. Our meagre sources of heat were the gas cooker, electric fires and one lukewarm radiator, linked to a solid fuel boiler that heated the water but little else.

'Why are you jigging about?'

'I want to go to the toilet – I'll just wait to the end of this programme.'

'Go – go now before you wet yourself.'

I was clearly annoying my brother.

You needed nerves of steel to run the route from the warmish room, where our family of five watched *Crossroads* and collectively added to the welcome fug, to upstairs and the single loo. Cut adrift from the bathroom, the toilet was its own icy box. Not a place to linger. Up, down, pee, dab, up, down, run.

When I think of that house now it seems always to be cold, ice forming inside the panes and tears of condensation mopped up by old towels tucked into the sills.

But those windows had one advantage. All that weathering had warped some of them. The angled window by the front door was about three feet high, topped with a small pane. Twisted by endless damp, this window was difficult to close and occasionally we worried about burglars. Tapping it

Yvana Reeves

meant eventually the stay would pop off its catch. Then you could reach down to lift the handle on the bigger window. From the front step, splayed outwards to provide an open porch, you could just get a leg up onto the sill and clinging on, reach to tap the bent window frame. Not easy, but when it's gone midnight and your dad has locked the front door to teach you a lesson, again, it turns out to be a godsend.

Tap, tap, tap, creak. Reaching down, opening the bigger window, just big enough to let you through, you could wriggle through the lace curtains and drop into the front room.

'Shhh, be careful,' I said to my boyfriend, Keith. Close cropped hair, intense blue eyes and a cub reporter for the local newspaper in Maidenhead.

'I'm trying to give you a lift up, make it easier. Put your left leg there.'

'Well – be careful where you put your hands!' Trying not to giggle or make a sound that would bring my dad down, we would eventually succeed in getting me in.

Keith would return to his beloved Hillman Hunter and drive off, content, I imagine, to go over our evening date, which normally ended with a bit of slap and tickle on the car's front bench seat.

Crouching in the grey shadows while he left, I would wait and listen, getting my night sight. I would close the windows quietly and make my way carefully through the room, out into the hall, hang up my coat gently and count my way up the stairs, avoiding the third step altogether as it creaked, and pausing on the very outer part of the seventh one, which gurgled strangely in the middle. Still no sound. OK, go.

Not a time to wash or pee. I would take off my outer clothes and slide into the cold bed and sleep as soon as I warmed, smiling at my latest adventure.

Dad was in his forties when I was courting Keith and discovering all about love. He lived another fifty years, but we never discussed whether he knew exactly what my method of breaking and entering had been. I like to think Dad was cutting me a little slack. ⁄⁄

Yvana Reeves

Haywain

If I think of paradise
I smell warm, scythed hay
coming from Italian fields
backed by mountains, holding
secrets of partisans and hope.

I picture the swaying haywain,
no British horse but a donkey,
pulling the ever-toppling load
which never falls, except for
flyaway golden straws.

Clinging on top, wriggling in,
cousins play and dream
as warm sun beats down on
bare-topped, brown bodies
on the slow, steady pull home.

Paradise is a memory
of childhood and belonging,
sticky saved cold risotto,
watered rough red wine
carried to haymakers with love. ⫽

Yvana Reeves

Other anthologies and collections available from Stairwell Books

For further information please contact rose@stairwellbooks.com
www.stairwellbooks.co.uk
@stairwellbooks

Lightning Source UK Ltd.
Milton Keynes UK
UKHW022134171121
394111UK00010B/372